JOHNS HOPKINS
Centennial Portrait of a University

by Robert P. Sharkey

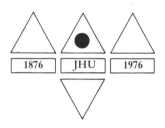

1975
The Johns Hopkins University
Baltimore, Maryland

Published by the Office of University
Publications, The Johns Hopkins
University, 1975.

Library of Congress catalog card number 74-34210

Introduction

The genesis of this work goes back to 1960–61 when I was working as administrative assistant to President Milton S. Eisenhower. At that time I wrote a brief history of the University, which was published under the title *Johns Hopkins: Portrait of a University*.

Early in 1973, long after I thought this work had passed into oblivion, Ross Jones, the very competent and energetic Vice-President for University Affairs, suggested that I update this essay in connection with the upcoming centennial observance. After some consideration I agreed, thinking that the updating, if done to scale, would require only a few weeks of time. What began to appall me in the summer of 1973 when I began to do some preliminary research was the fact that any treatment of the enormously complex development of Johns Hopkins over the past two decades which even pretended to present an accurate picture would require far more time, pages, and effort than I had originally anticipated.

What I decided to do, after consideration, was to concentrate on the University's history since Dr. Eisenhower assumed the presidency in 1956 in order to present at least a partially adequate description of what Johns Hopkins is as it enters upon its centennial era. The title, *Johns Hopkins: Centennial Portrait of a University*, is really more accurate than in the earlier version. What is presented here is a treatment of the contemporary University preceded by a brief and hopefully accurate historical sketch. Some readers may find the foreground a bit too tedious and detailed and the background somewhat sketchy. I can only offer the solace that the earlier history of Johns Hopkins has been exhaustively treated in a number of scholarly works available to the interested reader.

In addition to Vice-President Ross Jones who has been most helpful, I should like to offer my thanks to Dr. Ferdinand Hamburger, Jr., Director of Centennial Planning, who has been a constant source of cooperation and support; to Mrs. Mary Johnson of the Office of Centennial Planning, without whose timely encouragement this work would never have been completed; and to Mrs. Kathryn Jacob, University Archivist, who has done much thankless work in chasing down facts and figures and who is also responsible for the most useful appendix. I should also like to thank those who have read portions of the manuscript and have offered criticisms, including: President Emeritus Milton S. Eisenhower; Deans Emeriti G. Wilson Shaffer of the Homewood Schools, Thomas B. Turner of the School of Medicine, Ernest B. Stebbins of the School of Hygiene and Public Health, and Francis O. Wilcox of the School of Advanced International Studies; Registrar Emeritus Irene Davis; and Robert Scott, Director of Athletics. Any errors which occur in this work are, of course, my own responsibility.

In my opinion it would be impossible for any individual to truly understand even 25 percent of what goes on in The Johns Hopkins University in any single day. I trust that what follows will be understood with that *caveat* in mind.

Robert P. Sharkey

Washington, D.C., August, 1974

The long history of higher education in the Western world is studded with a series of important and memorable events. The founding of the Universities of Paris and Bologna in the twelfth century and the later establishment of Oxford and Cambridge obviously fall into this category. The year 1636 will always be associated with the beginnings of collegiate education in the American colonies. In this same category of notable events of germinal significance, historians of higher education include the establishment of The Johns Hopkins University in 1876.

It seems almost certain that the modern concept of the university would have evolved eventually in the United States if the institution bearing the name of Johns Hopkins had never existed. It is nonetheless true that Johns Hopkins was the pioneer university in this country and that it set the pace and established the standards for a host of institutions which followed. There were institutions in the United States which termed themselves universities prior to 1876. Some had even awarded the degree of doctor of philosophy. The truth of the matter was, however, that even the strongest and most prestigious of these institutions were really colleges rather than universities in the modern sense. They were devoted to passing on, largely by rote, the accumulated wisdom and folly of the ages. President Eliot, of Harvard, testified in 1902 that "the graduate school of Harvard University, started feebly in 1870 and 1871, did not thrive, until the example of Johns Hopkins forced our

Faculty to put their strength into the development of our instruction for graduates. And what was true of Harvard was true of every other university in the land which aspired to create an advanced school of arts and sciences."

Like most great institutions, The Johns Hopkins University was the result of a favorable conjunction of men, money, and circumstances. The proximate cause of its establishment was the generosity of a Maryland Quaker, whose wisdom and vision entitle him to a high rank in the annals of philanthropy.

Born in Anne Arundel County, Maryland, in 1795 on a tobacco plantation owned by his father, Johns Hopkins left the ancestral acres at the age of seventeen to work for his uncle, who conducted a wholesale grocery and commission business in Baltimore. By the time he was twenty-four, Johns had established a mercantile house of his own, laying the foundation for his own prosperity as well as acquiring a reputation for unusual energy, intelligence, and business acumen. Fortune smiled on the young Quaker, and he never seemed to suffer unduly from the vagaries of the business cycle which prostrated many of his commercial rivals. Early realizing the vital importance of transportation from the port of Baltimore to the interior, he was a dynamic force in the development of the Baltimore and Ohio Railroad. Investing heavily in its stock, he became a director of the road in 1847 and chairman of its powerful finance committee in 1855. On several occasions the immense private fortune of Johns Hopkins was employed to bolster the credit of the railroad in times of financial stress.

Johns Hopkins never married. This fact probably influenced him when he came, in the twilight of his life, to contemplate the disposition of his great fortune. Exactly how Mr. Hopkins came to his decision is shrouded in conjecture. He had always kept his own counsel and did not actively seek advice from his contemporaries. Whatever his inner deliberations, he had decided by the summer of 1867 to give effect to his decision. In August of that year twelve citizens of Baltimore formed at his request a corporation known as "The Johns Hopkins University," whose purpose was simply "the promotion of education in the State of Maryland." Twelve trustees were named, four of them related to Mr. Hopkins and others his friends and neighbors. By another similar act there was incorporated "The Johns Hopkins

Hospital," which also had twelve trustees, all but two of whom were also members of the board of the University.

When Johns Hopkins died late in 1873, his will disclosed that he had provided generously for these two great projects. The great bulk of his fortune, a sum amounting to more than $7 million, was divided equally between the university and the hospital destined to bear his name. This was the greatest single philanthropic bequest which had occurred in the United States up until that time.

△ △ △

Although the founder was quite specific in outlining his designs for the Hospital, he was virtually silent on the subject of his desires for the University. Only two paragraphs in the will gave expression to his wishes. The trustees were forbidden to use the principal of the bequest for buildings or current expenses; they were directed to provide certain free scholarships, and they were advised to hold and administer wisely the vast portfolio of Baltimore and Ohio Railroad stock, which constituted a considerable portion of the founder's fortune.

One other wish had been made clear by Johns Hopkins before he died. In a letter written to the Hospital trustees in 1873, he asserted his "wish and purpose that the institution should ultimately form a part of the medical school of that university for which I have made ample provision by my will." The inscrutable mind of the founder leaves little evidence as to whether he truly understood the revolutionary nature of his expressed purpose, for in this letter he did nothing less than outline the form of a hospital which would bring medical science to the bedside, and a medical school which would, from the beginning, emphasize the importance of research and clinical experience.

Very wisely did the founder leave the implementation of his grand design for a university to a carefully selected board of trustees. These men were not professional educators but rather, like Johns Hopkins himself, men of affairs—lawyers, merchants, and bankers. They possessed a largeness of outlook, a lack of prejudice in educational matters, and a willingness to give weight to the best available expert advice. In retrospect, the wisdom of this first board of trustees seems most remarkable. In the course of making important decisions as to the exact form the new university should take, they conferred with a number of distinguished educators, including Charles W. Eliot, of Harvard; Andrew D. White, of Cornell; and James B. Angell, of Michigan. The board also collected a number of published works in the field of higher education, a further indication that the trustees had every desire to make their decisions on the basis of the best available knowledge.

Expert testimony had revealed the fact that among educators there was no felt need for just another college like the four hundred already existing in the United States. There was, however, an almost unanimous desire for what President Angell of Michigan described as "a great graduate university" that would strike out boldly toward new frontiers of knowledge. In the opinion of Angell, Eliot, White, and others, there was only one man in the country entirely competent to direct such a task. That man was Daniel Coit Gilman, at that time president of the University of California.

△ △ △

There can be little doubt that Dr. Gilman was the best possible choice for the presidency of the new Johns Hopkins University. He brought to the task a cultured and creative mind and a firmness of purpose combined with a degree of vision unmatched in the history of American higher education. When Gilman began his work in Baltimore, he was at the peak of his powers. His previous experience as teacher, scholar, and administrator at Yale, as *de facto* superintendent of schools in New Haven, and finally as president of the University of California had well fitted him for the role of educational statesman. Gilman journeyed to Baltimore in December, 1874. In his conferences with the board of trustees he explained that he would not want to create simply another college, but rather a university which would assume the task of promoting creative thought and scholarship at the highest levels. In this desire the trustees heartily concurred and formally elected him the first president of The Johns Hopkins University.

Gilman was authorized by the trustees to travel extensively in this country and in Europe in order to obtain the best advice available in the field of higher education. Traveling to Europe in the summer of 1875, the new president conferred with a large number of men distinguished in the arts and sciences both in England and on the Continent. When he returned, he was even more fixed in his purpose to create a great new institution comparable to the greatest universities in Europe, yet distinctively American in its essential nature.

The trustees agreed with the president in placing scant emphasis on the bricks-and-mortar requirements of higher education. The faculty, however, was of crucial importance, for it was by attracting professors of great ability—paying them adequately, surrounding them by selected students of promise, and providing them with time to pursue their researches—that Gilman hoped to create a great university.

The first faculty consisted of five carefully chosen university professors: Basil L. Gildersleeve, in Greek; James J. Sylvester, in mathematics; Ira Remsen, in chemistry; Henry A. Rowland, in physics; and Henry N. Martin, in biology. Because Gilman had always thought that The Johns Hopkins University should include undergraduate instruction as well as graduate work, Charles D. Morris was employed as collegiate professor of Greek and Latin. Gilman's wisdom in selecting this first faculty was amply demonstrated over the years, for all of the University professors soon achieved distinction in the world of learning.

The attractions of the new University were strong, for there came to Johns Hopkins in the fall of 1876 a group of twenty graduate students of exceptional promise. In this first group of Fellows are found such names as Herbert B. Adams, in history; Henry C. Adams, in political science; Charles R. Lanman, in philology; Harmon N. Morse, in chemistry; and Josiah Royce, in philosophy. Thirteen of this original group later held professorships in American colleges and universities; two were scientists in the government service; three more were well-recognized private scholars; and one, Walter Hines Page, later became Ambassador to England.

△ △ △

The influence of The Johns Hopkins University in its early years can hardly be overemphasized. In the few unpretentious

5

buildings on North Howard Street in what is now downtown Baltimore, there gathered either as faculty or students such notables as Frederick Jackson Turner, Charles S. Peirce, Woodrow Wilson, G. Stanley Hall, A. Marshall Elliott, Sidney Lanier, Simon Newcomb, and John Dewey. It was a period of pioneering excitement—a time, as Josiah Royce put it, "wherein 'twas bliss to be alive."

Gilman's creation of a university which would regard knowledge as a dynamic living force in human affairs rather than as a revered historical monument was a tremendous success, because it fulfilled a very great need. By the middle of the third decade of the twentieth century, a great number of universities in the United States offered programs of advanced study similar to those at Johns Hopkins. The germinal influence of the Baltimore institution at this time was nonetheless striking. Of the 1,440 persons who had received the various Hopkins doctorates in the course of fifty years (exclusive of medicine), nearly 1,000 were serving on the faculties of other educational institutions. Of the 1,000 most eminent American men of science at that time, 246, or nearly one-quarter, were Hopkins men. Of the 221 members of the National Academy of Sciences, 41, or more than 18 percent, were either members of the Hopkins faculty or had been trained at the University.

△ △ △

The Hopkins influence has always been greatly fostered through the medium of publications. Gilman well understood the importance of this, and almost from the beginning he took steps to see that the results of his faculty's investigations would be broadcast to the world. The first effort in this direction was the University's sponsorship of the *American Journal of Mathematics*, the pioneer American publication in the field. This was followed by the *American Chemical Journal*, which issued fifty volumes before it was taken over by the *Journal* of the American Chemical Society. In rapid succession there appeared the *American Journal of Philology*, the *Johns Hopkins University Studies in Historical and Political Science*, and *Modern Language Notes*. With the exception of the *American Chemical Journal*, all of these publications are still sponsored by the University today. Another significant medium of publication over the years has been the Johns Hopkins Press. Dating its establishment from 1878, it is the oldest continuing university press in the United States. It has published more than 2,400 works written by eminent scholars in a host of different fields.

I t had been understood from the beginning that The Johns Hopkins University would not be limited to the Faculty of Philosophy. The founder, the trustees, and the first president had all envisaged the establishment of a Faculty of Medicine. President Gilman and his trustees proceeded with this project carefully, for they realized that the lowly state of nineteenth-century American medical education demanded the same kind of hard-headed yet creative vision in launching a new medical school that had proved so successful in the earlier experiment with the Faculty of Philosophy.

Much depended upon the completion of The Johns Hopkins Hospital, for Gilman agreed completely with the conception of the founder that the medical school and the Hospital should be strongly interdependent. As the various buildings of the Hospital drew near to completion on their North Broadway site in east Baltimore, planning for the medical school shifted into high gear. As early as 1884, Dr. William H. Welch, who was destined to become the greatest medical statesman America has produced, accepted the position of professor of pathology at the University.

Since The Johns Hopkins Hospital planned to open its doors in the spring of 1889, it was now judicious to make other appointments. Dr. William Osler, Dr. Howard A. Kelly, and Dr. William S. Halsted had already accepted positions in the Hospital as physician-in-chief, gynecologist, and surgeon, respectively. Each of these was now appointed professor of the corresponding department in the University. These, together with Welch, were the famous "four doctors" who played such a great role in revolutionizing medical training in the United States.

The actual establishment of the School of Medicine* was delayed for a number of years because of the precarious financial position of the University in the late 1880's. Meanwhile, as early as 1877, steps had been taken by Gilman to create in the undergraduate college of the University the first premedical course in America.

The crucial financial problem was substantially solved in 1892 by the generous gifts of Miss Mary Garrett of Baltimore and others, who provided nearly a half-million dollars upon the condition that women would be admitted to the new school on the same terms as men. This condition was accepted by the trustees of the University, who announced their intention of opening the School of Medicine in the fall of 1893.

The "four doctors" already provided the nucleus for a Faculty of Medicine. William Henry Welch was selected as the first dean of the school, and other appointments followed: Franklin P. Mall, as professor of anatomy; John J. Abel, to fill the chair of pharmacology; and William H. Howell, as professor of physiology.

△ △ △

In establishing a collegiate premedical course, Gilman made clear his conviction that the new School of Medicine should admit only superior students who were thoroughly grounded in the fundamental sciences antecedent to the study of medicine. This was a radically new idea, for, as Welch pointed out in 1893, no American medical school then required for admission "knowledge approaching that necessary for entrance into the freshman class of a respectable college." Fears were expressed that a drastic raising of standards of admission to the new medical school would result in a dearth of students, but such did not prove to be the case. Superior students were attracted to The Johns Hopkins School of Medicine simply because it did maintain high standards. In setting this precedent, Johns Hopkins made a significant contribution toward raising the general level of American medical education.

* The institution was actually known as The Johns Hopkins Medical School until 1924 when it became the School of Medicine. The latter designation is used throughout to avoid confusion.

Within a few years a basic curriculum had been established. Building upon an undergraduate education which included training in basic science areas such as chemistry and biology, medical students in their first two years were required to develop a broad and deep understanding of subjects fundamental to clinical medicine such as anatomy, physiology, pharmacology, and pathology. In the third and fourth years, students left the lecture halls and laboratories to gain practical training and experience in the wards and clinics of The Johns Hopkins Hospital. In making medical students in their clinical years an integral part of the staff of the Hospital, the School of Medicine embarked upon a course which was novel in the 1890's, but which is accepted today as virtually essential for any medical school worthy of the name.

One of the great contributions of The Johns Hopkins School of Medicine in conjunction with the Hospital was the promulgation of the "full-time" principle. As early as 1884, nine years before the School of Medicine actually opened its doors, the University Board of Trustees made it clear that appointments to professorships of the preclinical medical sciences would be made strictly on a full-time basis. This meant that the holders of preclinical chairs would be required to devote themselves entirely to teaching and research without any of the distractions of private practice. Although this principle is taken for granted in all first-rate medical schools today, it was considered a distinct innovation at the time, and Johns Hopkins can take credit for being the first such institution to place all its preclinical professors on a full-time basis.

△ △ △

In 1914, after years of debate and self-searching analysis, the School of Medicine took the dramatic step of placing its main clinical chairs on a full-time basis. The medical faculty was by no means unanimous as to the advisability of such a policy. Doctors Osler and Kelly were decidedly opposed to a principle which they thought would convert clinicians into austere scientists largely removed from a humanizing doctor-patient relationship. Only Welch with all his prestige and influence could successfully launch such an experiment. He did not move quickly on such an important matter, but having been convinced finally of the validity of the full-time principle for the clinical sciences, his support was decisive. Aided by a large grant of funds from the General Education Board, full-time professorships were first established in medicine, surgery, pediatrics, and eventually in other departments. The example set by Johns Hopkins in this case was again influential, for many progressive medical schools have tended ever since to gravitate toward adoption of the full-time principle.

Beginning with a faculty of fifteen, including nine professors and six associates in 1893, the growth of the School of Medicine was steady. Subjects of instruction which had been included in originally existing departments were eventually established as separate organizations in the following order: Obstetrics, 1899; Physiological Chemistry, 1908; Pediatrics, 1909; Psychiatry, 1910; Ophthalmology, 1925; The History of Medicine, 1929; Preventive Medicine, 1941.

Over the years the contributions of Johns Hopkins to the science of medicine have been so numerous that volumes would be required to tell the story. Many of these have first seen the light of day in such publications as the *Bulletin of the Johns Hopkins Hospital,* a joint enterprise of the Hospital and the School of Medicine, and the *Journal of Experimental Medicine,* which had its genesis at Johns Hopkins in 1896. Beginning with Sir William Osler's great work, *Principles and Practice of Medicine,* and Dr. Howard Kelly's influential *Operative Gynecology,* a stream of basic medical texts in fields such as obstetrics, pediatrics, pathology, and physiology has continued to emanate from east Baltimore, extending the influence of the School of Medicine throughout the world.

Five medical graduates of Hopkins have achieved the summit of scientific eminence, the Nobel prize: Joseph Erlanger, G. H. Whipple, H. S. Gasser, Peyton Rous, and H. K. Hartline. Since its establishment the School of Medicine has produced hundreds of full professors and several thousand other teachers who have served on the faculties of more than fifty other medical schools. In several instances Hopkins-trained doctors have been instrumental in the establishment of other distinguished medical schools. Thus has the record amply justified the faith of that small group of devoted men who launched a great experiment in the fall of 1893.

The second decade of the twentieth century witnessed another pioneering venture of The Johns Hopkins University. In 1915, at the behest of the General Education Board, Dr. William H. Welch and Mr. Wycliffe Rose prepared a report which took cognizance of the lack of educational facilities in the fields of public health and hygiene and recommended the establishment of an institute to be maintained within the framework of some existing university. The result of this report was a substantial grant by the Rockefeller Foundation for a new institution which was to become a part of The Johns Hopkins University. This was the genesis of the School of Hygiene and Public Health, which, in the words of Dr. John C. French, "is the lengthened shadow of William H. Welch."

The School has fully maintained the Hopkins tradition of dynamic innovation. Beginning its work in the fall of 1918 with Dr. Welch as first director, the new institution soon gathered a faculty of eminent teachers and researchers in such fields as bacteriology, immunology, physiological hygiene, chemical hygiene, biochemistry, and medical zoology. In succeeding years departments were added in other fields: epidemiology, public health administration, biostatistics, environmental medicine, microbiology, pathobiology, and sanitary engineering.

By 1922 it was apparent that the School of Hygiene and Public Health was a great success. In recognition of this fact the Rockefeller Foundation now provided a substantial endowment fund in addition to a grant of $1 million for construction. The new home of the school was occupied in 1926. Facing on Wolfe Street at the corner of Monument, the School of Hygiene and Public Health became a part of the Johns Hopkins medical complex in east Baltimore. Its influence over the past fifty years has been very great in this country and in many foreign nations. In this period the School has trained more than half of the state directors or commissioners of health. Students have been drawn from all the states of the Union and from more than sixty foreign countries. More than 160 have become ministers of health or chief medical officers in their home countries. Of the representatives of the sixty-six nations that met in

New York in 1946 to draft the constitution of the World Health Organization, thirty-four were graduates of The Johns Hopkins School of Hygiene and Public Health.

△ △ △

The twenty-fifth anniversary of the University, which was celebrated in February, 1902, was an occasion both for joy and sorrow—joy that the University was a great success and now enjoyed world-wide renown, and sorrow that President Gilman had reached the end of his years of fruitful service at Hopkins. Delegates to the celebration came from more than eighty educational institutions in the United States and Canada. Tributes to the accomplishments of Gilman and his colleagues were paid unstintingly by such notables as Presidents Charles W. Eliot of Harvard, Arthur Twining Hadley of Yale, and William Rainey Harper of the University of Chicago. In expressing the appreciation of the alumni, Professor Woodrow Wilson of Princeton asserted that the men of Johns Hopkins had taken from the University "an ideal which has lifted their lives to a plane they might not otherwise have attained; an ideal . . . of the service of truth not only, but of the service through truth, of the country of which they are citizens."

This celebration was also the occasion for the inauguration of Ira Remsen as second president of the University. Long famed for his teaching and research in the field of chemistry, Remsen had been a member of the original faculty of the University and a close friend of President Gilman. Unlike Gilman, President Remsen had little taste for university administration. His presidency, which lasted until 1913, was essentially a period of consolidation.

In these years the normal course of undergraduate instruction leading to the A.B. degree was extended from three to four years. The three-year course, instituted by Gilman, had been based on the assumption that students admitted to the University would have received an extremely high quality of secondary instruction. The apparent deficiencies of school preparation in these years led to the adoption in 1906 of the more conventional four-year course.

△ △ △

Almost from the beginning it had been realized that collegiate and graduate instruction would not be continued indefinitely on the downtown Howard Street campus. As the nineteenth century waned and the surrounding neighborhood began to deteriorate, a move to a permanent suburban location became ever more desirable. The difficulty lay in acquiring a proper site. This problem was eventually solved through a combination of philanthropy and intricate negotiations. In this process Mr. William Keyser played a leading part, and he was aided in his design by other civic-minded Baltimoreans, including his cousin Mr. William Wyman, Mr. Samuel Keyser, Mr. W. H. Buckler, Mr. Julian L. White, and Mr. Francis M. Jencks. Together these men presented the University with the beautiful tract of land in north Baltimore that is now the Homewood Campus.

Influenced by the fact that the new campus had been for more than a century the site of Homewood House, a very fine example of the Georgian style and originally the country home of the son of Charles Carroll, of Carrollton, the president and the board of trustees decided to conform to this style of architecture in planning new buildings. The first structure to be erected for purposes of instruction was Gilman Hall, which was dedicated in May, 1915. Since that time twenty-five buildings have been constructed at Homewood, providing facilities for undergraduate and graduate instruction in the arts, sciences, and engineering.

President Remsen resigned the presidency of the University in 1913 for reasons of ill health. After careful consideration of available candidates by the trustees, it was announced that the third president of the University would be Frank Johnson Goodnow, a political scientist with a long record of public service to both domestic and foreign governments.

Shortly before the inauguration of President Goodnow, the first laboratory of the Johns Hopkins School of Engineering had been completed at Homewood. The need for such a school within the State of Maryland had long been realized, and the occasion of the University's move to Homewood appeared to many public-spirited citizens to present an excellent opportunity for launching this important project. The matter was presented to the State Legislature, and a committee of lawmakers was appointed to confer with the trustees. The result of these deliberations was an appropriation by the Legislature of $600,000 for buildings and equipment and an annual appropriation of $50,000, which was to be used largely for scholarships for residents of Maryland.

The first faculty in engineering was organized in 1913. John B. Whitehead, already professor of applied electricity in the Department of Physics, became professor of electrical engineering. Dr. Whitehead also became secretary of the new school and in 1920 its first dean. Other appointments were Charles J. Tilden, called from the University of Michigan to be professor of civil engineering, and Carl C. Thomas, of the University of Wisconsin, to be professor of mechanical engineering. In due course other departments of instruction were established and by 1932–33 the school had an enrollment of 395 of whom 36 were registered for graduate work.

President Gilman had warned that the University must beware lest it "impart a knowledge of methods rather than principles." This advice has always been regarded seriously at Johns Hopkins, and it has been felt that it has particular relevance to a school of engineering. From the time of its inception, the school placed far more emphasis upon the basic sciences and cultural subjects than was the custom in the vast majority of technological institutions. That this emphasis has increased rather than decreased in recent years will be made clear further along in this narrative.

△ △ △

From its earliest years, Johns Hopkins had recognized a special responsibility to bring educational opportunities to the residents of Baltimore, at first through public lectures initiated by President Gilman, and later through non-credit "lesson courses" which were instituted about 1890. In 1909 a separate division of the University, originally known as College Courses for Teachers and later as the College for Teachers, was organized and provided instruction of collegiate grade in the field of professional education and also in liberal arts subjects.

An influx of industrial workers into Baltimore during World War I greatly heightened the demand for programs of study which could be pursued at night. Beginning in 1916, night courses for technical workers and evening courses in business economics were offered. At the end of the war it was discovered that there was still a considerable demand for such courses, and the enrollment in the night program continued to grow. In 1947, all of the evening offerings of the University were consolidated into a new division called McCoy College in honor of John W. McCoy, an early benefactor of Johns Hopkins. In 1965 the name of this division was changed simply to the Evening College. In 1973–74 it enrolled more than 5,000 students in 328 different credit and non-credit courses.

One of President Goodnow's greatest services to the University lay in his wise management of finances during a period of rapid expansion. During his fifteen-year tenure of office, the income of the University increased from a half-million to nearly $2.5 million annually, while the value of the plant and endowment grew from $10 million to nearly $40 million. In the final year of the Goodnow administration, 68 percent of the expenditures of the University went for salaries, a record which indicated that the University tradition which valued men more highly than buildings and appurtenances was still maintained.

Reluctantly the trustees accepted President Goodnow's resignation, which took effect on July 1, 1929. His successor was Joseph Sweetman Ames, who was continuously associated with Johns Hopkins as student, professor, dean, provost, president, and president emeritus for a period of sixty years. A student of Rowland, Dr. Ames was highly regarded for his contributions to the science of physics. He was a member of the National Academy of Sciences and in 1919–20 served as president of the American Physical Society. An expert in the basic principles of aviation, he served for nearly a quarter-century as a member of the National Advisory Committee for Aeronautics. Having served the University in several administrative capacities since 1924, Dr. Ames, although nearly sixty-five years of age when he took office, brought to the presidency a wide range of useful experience.

As was the case with most universities, Johns Hopkins had to lay aside plans for new activities in the early 1930's in order to wrestle with the financial problems of the Great Depression. As income fell, deficits mounted steadily. President Ames had the onerous duty of enforcing a policy of extreme frugality. Realizing the gravity of the situation, the faculties of the University met and agreed to a voluntary cut of 10 percent in their salaries. These and other measures helped, but the deficits continued, amounting to more than $183,000 during President Ames' last year in office.

It was during these years that the University began to chart a course which was to lead eventually to a de-commercialization of athletics. President Ames felt strongly that it was "most improper for an institution of learning itself to charge admission fees to athletic contests." Although the financial straits of the University in the early thirties did not permit a sudden abolition of gate receipts, these years did mark a swing in that direction. In 1937 the step was taken, and for more than thirty years no admission fees were collected for sports events. Today, although the general public (but not faculty, students, and administrators) is charged for admission to football and lacrosse games, the Hopkins athletic program is still permeated with ideals of amateurism and non-commercialization which seem almost quaint by modern standards.

△ △ △

When President Ames retired in 1935 at the age of seventy, it was announced that his successor would be Isaiah Bowman, at that time director of the American Geographical Society of New York. As a distinguished geographer he had served the government on several occasions—as chief territorial advisor to Woodrow Wilson at the Versailles peace conference, as chairman of the National Research Council, and as vice-chairman of the Science Advisory Board. Throughout his life Dr. Bowman was a productive scholar, publishing nine books and a large number of articles, mostly in his chosen field of geography.

The new president inherited many of the financial problems which had plagued his predecessor. While adhering to a policy of strict economy, the University launched a fund-raising campaign which resulted in pledges of approximately a half-million dollars. The success of this effort, combined with some improvement in investment income, made it possible to meet impending deficits with greater confidence.

Throughout his presidency Dr. Bowman placed particular emphasis upon the importance of the undergraduate college to the health of the University as a whole. In 1925, President Goodnow had announced a plan of development which looked forward to the day when Johns Hopkins should "cease to give instruction in most of the subjects now taught in the first years of college." The plan envisaged combining "the work of the last two college years with what is now spoken of as graduate work, applying to all this work essentially the methods and standards that are applicable to . . . graduate work." When fully operative, students working under the Goodnow plan would not receive bachelor's degrees but would instead aim directly for one of the higher degrees.

Although approved by the trustees of the University, the Goodnow plan was never successful. It proved impossible to find properly qualified students who wished to transfer into graduate programs of study at the end of the sophomore year. It was also found that very few students wished to bypass the A.B. degree in the course of working toward the doctorate. However sound logically and pedagogically, the plan proved not to be well adapted to the actual needs or desires of undergraduate students.

In his inaugural address Dr. Bowman asserted his "resolute intention to advance the interest, improve the quality, and bring to a high state of efficiency the Johns Hopkins College of Arts and Sciences." This declaration did much to quiet the fears of alumni, many of whom had been concerned about the more negative aspects of the Goodnow plan. At the same time the new president emphasized the importance of advanced study, pointing out that the graduate school was "the most valuable, most expensive, and least understood intellectual enterprise of a university." He urged continuing efforts to obtain support for the kind of education that aims at high attainments by the few rather than mediocrity for the many.

△ △ △

As the decade of the thirties waned, the portents from Europe became increasingly ominous. Months before the United States was actually involved in the conflict, the University was rendering service to the national defense effort. College level courses aimed at the needs of various industrial plants were offered on a day and night basis, and the engineering laboratories were kept in use six days a week, winter and summer.

With the coming of war the tempo of University activity increased. War research at Johns Hopkins was so complex and varied that a volume would not suffice to tell the full story. Techniques for the manufacture of some critical materials used in the building of the atomic bomb were developed under the direction of Hopkins chemists. Another highly secret project had as its aim the use of infrared rays as a detection device. In the School of Medicine still another Hopkins task force coordinated the nation-wide effort to find a synthetic substitute for the anti-malarial drug, quinine. In the years 1941-45 the University participated either directly or indirectly in about one hundred research projects related to the war effort. In addition to this, some 4,500 Johns Hopkins graduates, students, and faculty served in the armed forces of the nation. One hundred twenty-two of these sacrificed their lives in defense of their country.

A special project deriving from the war effort deserves mention here inasmuch as it evolved over the years into a permanent division of the University. In 1942, Johns Hopkins was requested by the Office of Scientific Research and Development to undertake research looking to the development of what has come to be called the radio-proximity or VT (variable-time) fuze. Operating under conditions of profound secrecy, a laboratory was established and a staff assembled in Silver Spring, Maryland. Work went forward on a crash basis, and by the fall of 1942, the VT fuze had been perfected to the point that its manufacture could be turned over to industry. The success of the VT was decisive and dramatic. In the Pacific the fuze greatly increased the effectiveness of naval antiaircraft fire. It was spectacularly successful when used against the V–1 "buzz bombs" in Europe. In the Battle of the Bulge, artillery was largely able to stem the enemy advance by employing VT-fuzed shells over roads and foxholes, which offered little protection against air bursts.

In the postwar years this facility continued to operate in Silver Spring as the Applied Physics Laboratory of The Johns Hopkins University, under contract with the Department of the Navy. In 1954, the larger part of APL activities were centered in a group of new buildings located in Howard County, Maryland. Since that time the Laboratory has concentrated primarily on national defense problems and investigations of outer space. A spectacular achievement of APL scientists was the successful launching of the Transit navigational satellite in April, 1960. The Laboratory today employs a total of more than 2,500 people, of whom more than 800 are classified as senior professional staff.

△ △ △

Not the least of the services of Johns Hopkins men during World War II was the contribution of President Bowman. He served the Department of State as special advisor to Secretaries Hull and Stettinius, traveling with the latter to London in 1944 for an important conference with British government officials. He was a member of the American delegation to the Dumbarton Oaks Conference and later served as advisor to the Secretary of State at the San Francisco Conference, which established the United Nations.

The end of hostilities in 1945 brought a return of students to the nation's campuses. Like most universities, Johns Hopkins had suffered a loss of enrollment during the war years, although the total effect of this was somewhat mitigated by the presence of students attached to the Army Specialized Training Program. Whatever dearth there was, however, was soon corrected. In the academic year 1948–49, when the tide of veteran students was at its height, 1,794 undergraduates were registered. The number of graduate students in arts, sciences, and engineering totaled 957. At both the graduate and undergraduate levels, veterans predominated, lending an air of seriousness and purpose to the Homewood Campus.

Having presided over the affairs of the University for more than thirteen years of depression, war, and reconversion to peace, President Bowman relinquished his office in December, 1948. Among his memorials is a bronze bust placed at the entrance to the auditorium building, Shriver Hall.

△ △ △

In January, 1949, Detlev Wulf Bronk became the sixth president of Johns Hopkins. At the time of his appointment, Dr. Bronk was Johnson Professor of Biophysics and Director of the Eldridge Reeves Johnson Foundation for Medical Physics at the University of Pennsylvania. An eminent biophysicist, Dr. Bronk had served the scientific world and the government of the United States in many capacities.

The new president's scientific interests, together with a generous gift to the University, resulted in the establishment of the Thomas C. Jenkins Department of Biophysics in 1949. Endowed by Mrs. Jenkins in memory of her late husband, the department soon occupied a well-equipped new wing extending from the north side of the biology building, Mergenthaler Hall.

In 1950, the University assumed responsibility for a new division which had already achieved recognition in the increasingly important field of international relations. The School of Advanced International Studies, in Washington, D.C., had been originally established in 1943 by the Foreign Service Educational Foundation. Among those Foundation trustees who were active in the formation of the school were Representatives Christian A. Herter and Frances P. Bolton, Admiral Lewis L. Strauss, Mr. Paul H. Nitze, and Mr. Joseph C. Grew. Situated in the District of Columbia in close proximity to the departments of government with responsibilities in the field of foreign affairs, the School had been from its inception concerned with the training of specialists qualified to serve the government and private business organizations. In the late forties the decision was made to seek affiliation with a leading university. Overtures were made to Johns Hopkins, and the School was incorporated as a graduate division of the University. In 1955, the Bologna Center of the School was established in Italy. Attracting graduate students from the United States as well as many European countries, the Center has proven to be a highly successful experiment in international understanding.

△ △ △

In the summer of 1953, Dr. Bronk left the University to become president of the Rockefeller Institute. Unwilling to make a hasty appointment to such a crucial post and yet mindful of the needs for continuing direction from the top, the trustees persuaded Dr. Lowell J. Reed to come out of retirement to accept the presidency on an interim basis. Dr. Reed had been associated with The Johns Hopkins School of Hygiene and Public Health since 1918. In a long career of teaching and research he had made many vital contributions to the field of biostatistics. In 1937, he was appointed dean of the School of Hygiene and Public Health and, in 1946, vice-president of the University and the Hospital. Although he was sixty-seven years of age when he accepted the presidency, Dr. Reed brought to the office administrative ability combined with an extensive knowledge of the University.

The administration of President Reed witnessed the completion of three new buildings at Homewood. Shriver Hall, the gift of Alfred Jenkins Shriver of Baltimore, met a long-felt need for a modern auditorium as well as additional space for administrative offices. Ames Hall, a memorial to the fourth president of Johns Hopkins, provided classroom and laboratory space for the Departments of Electrical and Sanitary Engineering, Psychology, and Mathematics. Construction of this building was made possible through a generous appropriation by the State of Maryland. Finally, the completion of a large new dormitory made it possible for the first time to house on campus all out-of-town undergraduate students.

After many months of deliberation the trustees announced in the spring of 1956 that Dr. Reed's successor would be Dr. Milton S. Eisenhower, formerly president of the Pennsylvania State University. Dr. Eisenhower brought to the presidency of Johns Hopkins a wealth of experience in government and higher education. In the 1920's and 30's he had been associated with the Department of Agriculture, first as assistant to Secretary Jardine, and later as Director of Information and Land Use Coordinator. During World War II, he had served as director of the War Relocation Authority and as associate director of the Office of War Information. In 1943, Dr. Eisenhower returned to his native Kansas to become president of Kansas State University, acting in that capacity until 1950, when he accepted the call to Penn State. Over the years Dr. Eisenhower has devoted himself to a number of causes, serving as chairman of the U.S. National Commission for UNESCO, as a member of the President's Advisory Committee on Government Organization, as special ambassador, and personal representative of the President for Latin-American affairs, as a member of the National Advisory Committee on Inter-American Affairs, as chairman of the foundation-supported Committee on Government and Higher Education, and as a director of the Fund for Adult Education.

In his inaugural address as president of the University, February 22, 1957, Dr. Eisenhower asserted his conviction that Johns Hopkins "must occupy a uniquely creative role in the total complex of American higher education." Recognizing the desirability of diversity in higher education and the great necessity for publicly supported institutions, he emphasized the vital and continuing need for quality, declaring that "the independent university is in a favored position to set examples of excellence which make it easier for the public institutions to strive toward the same standards." Affirming his belief in the historic mission of Johns Hopkins to expand the area of man's knowledge, the new president asserted: "Our strength cannot be in numbers. It must be in excellence."

Dr. Eisenhower's first presidency had a duration of nearly eleven years—until the summer of 1967. These years were filled with events of great significance in defining the University's niche in the world of modern higher education. Because the developments of these years tended to set contours for the future, it is desirable to survey the most important of them in some detail.

△ △ △

When Dr. Eisenhower took over the reins of leadership in 1956, he soon discovered the precarious condition of the University's general health. Despite spectacular accomplishments during two World Wars and a Depression, despite the fact that the faculties of various divisions were among the most eminent in the world, the truth was that Johns Hopkins generally suffered from acute financial anemia. In thirty-two out of the forty-six years between 1910 and 1956 expenditures had exceeded income. Faculty salaries, once the highest in the nation, were no longer competitive with many other universities. Physical facilities had, in many cases, become outmoded and inadequate. At Homewood only one major academic building, Ames Hall, had been constructed in nearly twenty years. The needs of the Medical Institutions were equally great, since the only major facility which had been added in more than a quarter of a century was the Clinical Science building, occupied in 1954. Library facilities were increasingly inadequate as were the funds necessary to purchase the books and periodicals containing the vast annual increments in knowledge. Doctoral production was stagnant and many faculty posts were vacant due to lack of funds. Dr. Eisenhower faced up to these crucial problems in his inaugural address when he said: "We must enlarge and strengthen the faculty . . . raise the compensation of faculty members . . . strengthen the adviser program . . . improve physical facilities. . . . enter new fields of scholarship . . . and attract superior students."

The decade of Dr. Eisenhower's first presidency coincided with a period of history in which the federal government out of sheer necessity looked to the great public and private universities to provide the leadership required to maintain America's cherished reputation for supremacy in science and technology, a reputation which had been undermined by Russia's success with Sputnik I in 1957. During these years Johns Hopkins benefited enormously, not only from a stream of federal funds flowing primarily (but not entirely) into basic and applied science, but also from a heightened interest by foundations and individuals in the health of private higher education. This situation presented not only great opportunities, but also considerable dangers. Since its inception, Johns Hopkins had consciously chosen both smallness and excellence. In an era of increasing giantism in government, in the corporate world, and increasingly in higher education, how could a small and essentially elite institution, painfully in need of additional funding, possibly avoid the centrifugal pressures tending to force it into a variety of uncoordinated activities for which money might be available but which could be subversive of the essential mission of the University in teaching and basic research? How, as Dr. Eisenhower graphically put it, could Johns Hopkins avoid the peril of becoming "a multiversity connected only by a common plumbing system"?

Fortunately the leadership of Johns Hopkins in these crucial years ranked with the best in its history. Backed by an able and dedicated board of trustees whose chairman was Mr. Charles S. Garland, a distinguished Baltimore investment banker, Dr. Eisenhower brought to the presidency of the University a combination of qualities almost unique in the annals of American higher education. In a career encompassing more than thirty years of service at the highest levels of government and higher education, Dr. Eisenhower was noted for a capacity to view problems with singular clarity and from the broadest possible perspective. Because he was a warm, friendly, and enthusiastic person, be was able to communicate to students, faculty, alumni, and the public generally his own sense of the greatness to which Johns Hopkins should constantly aspire. His technique was not to drive but always to lead. Faculty members and students found themselves consulted by the president on a variety of important matters. What is more, they found themselves doing most of the talking as the president listened intently, taking everything in, making an occasional comment. This style of leadership contributed to a sense of participation on the part of the entire University community in the vital decision-making process.

△ △ △

In the area of finance and resource development the Eisenhower years were years of spectacular achievement. In every fiscal year from 1957 through 1967 the University operated within a balanced budget and was able to set aside substantial reserves. Income more than tripled in this period while the endowment fund nearly doubled, amounting at the end of fiscal 1966 to a total of approximately $150,000,000.

While financial anemia was giving way to rosy good health, the scale of the University's operations reflected to a large extent an ever increasing level of government and private support for programs of teaching and research. In fiscal 1957 University operating expenditures excluding the Applied Physics Laboratory (which was entirely supported by the federal government) amounted to $16.5 million. Nine years later for fiscal 1966 the figure had more than tripled to $54.8 million. Of this latter amount the government contributed slightly more than half, mostly to the programs of research in medicine, public health, and the physical and biological sciences. It was obvious that in many crucial areas of endeavor the University and the federal government had joined in an uneasy but nonetheless highly fruitful partnership.

To maintain the independence and integrity of a private university in such a situation was no easy matter. Its vital importance was underscored, however, when Dr. Eisenhower mounted a well-thought-out campaign to attract the support of alumni, business, friends, and private foundations. On September 25, 1960, newspapers across the nation featured the dramatic news that five privately supported American universities had received large unrestricted grants from the Ford Foundation. As one of the institutions selected to participate in this Special Program in Education, Johns Hopkins received an initial grant of $6 million, the largest single donation of funds for general purposes in the University's history. The objective of the program according to the president of the Ford Foundation was "to assist institutions in different regions of the country to reach and sustain a wholly new level of academic excellence, administrative effectiveness, and financial support." Among the criteria for selection were "excellence of leadership," "strength of constituency," "a tradition of scholarship," and "plans to move toward greater scholarly accomplishment." This grant was a powerful incentive to continuing development not only because the University was accorded the freedom to use the funds in light of its own needs and priorities, but also because it was a condition of the grant that Hopkins raise from other sources (not including government funds) two dollars for every one dollar contributed by the Ford Foundation. Friends of John Hopkins everywhere responded magnificently to this stimulus—so impressively, in fact, that the Ford Foundation soon announced another $6 million grant to the University on the same terms. By 1964 the job had been done. Twenty-four million dollars had been raised from private sources to match the $12 million provided by the Ford Foundation.

This is but the most spectacular example of the success of fund-raising efforts during the Eisenhower years. A total of more than $100 million was received in private gifts and grants during this decade. By 1967 private gift income was running at the rate of more than $10 million annually.

Financial health made possible the achievement of goals which would have seemed impossible a few years earlier. The improvement of faculty salaries had the highest priority since they had slipped badly in the years after World War II. With determined effort Hopkins moved from the mediocre "B" scale to the "A" or "AA" scale in some divisions as ranked by the American Association of University Professors. By 1966–67 an analysis indicated that Hopkins salaries ranked fourth among all American universities. Such a vast improvement provided the University with the necessary competitive edge in retaining its distinguished senior faculty and in attracting some of the best young minds in the academic world.

△ △ △

While the bricks and mortar requirements of education and research had never ranked particularly high in the Hopkins scale of values, it was becoming painfully obvious in the second half of the twentieth century that the conditions of Spartan simplicity in which Gilman and his little band of scholars had thrived were no longer consonant with the levels of achievement to which the University aspired. From the outset Dr. Eisenhower addressed his administration to the problem of rejuvenating the physical plant of each of the major academic divisions of Johns Hopkins. In the course of his presidency more than $50 million was spent on new buildings, an amount greater than the value of the entire plant in 1957.

At the Medical Institutions the sights and sounds of construction were rarely absent from the late fifties onward. Major projects (some of which were undertaken with the Hospital) included the Lowell J. Reed Residence Hall, the W. Barry Wood Basic Science Building, the Biophysics Building, the Children's Medical and Surgical Center, the Alan C. Woods Research Building of the Wilmer Institute, the Samuel W. Traylor Research Building, the Thomas B. Turner Auditorium, and three additional wings to the Main Building of the School of Hygiene and Public Health. There was also a considerable renovation of existing facilities, notably parts of the Pathology and Physiology buildings. In these years there was also constructed on property adjacent to the Medical Institutions the affiliated John F. Kennedy Institute for the Habilitation of the Mentally and Physically Handicapped Child. In addition a number of ancillary facilities were constructed in the immediate neighborhood, including an office-apartment building, the Sheraton-Baltimore Inn, the cooperative Hospital laundry, and a parking garage.

The needs at Homewood in 1956 were, if anything, even more critical than those of the Medical Institutions. Not all of these needs could be met during the Eisenhower administration, but the progress made was tremendous. For years the inadequacy of physical facilities in the sciences and engineering had given rise to increasing concern over the University's ability to maintain its traditional quality in scientific instruction and research. Much of the thrust of the building program of the early and mid-sixties was designed to remedy this situation. The physics building, Rowland Hall, was doubled in size, and a five-story wing was added to Mergenthaler Hall, which houses the Departments of Biology and Biophysics. To the north of Keyser Quadrangle, two handsome new buildings arose, Dunning Hall, housing various research activities of the Department of Chemistry, and Macaulay Hall, a memorial to long-time provost and vice-president, P. Stewart Macaulay, devoted to the oceanographic program of the Department of Earth and

Planetary Sciences. On Wyman Quadrangle, Barton Hall, named for former Board of Trustees chairman Carlyle Barton, was completed in 1962, providing greatly increased physical capability for work in radiation and electrical engineering.

The space and equipment requirements of social scientists and humanists are not nearly so great as those of scientists and engineers. Nonetheless, the needs of faculty and students in the fifteen departments embraced by these divisions were critical. Gilman Hall, the one significant physical facility servicing these departments, had been completed in 1915. It contained not only offices, classrooms, and various miscellaneous facilities, but, most significantly, it housed with ever-increasing inadequacy the library collections in the social sciences and the humanities. Since there was simply no more space for the annual accretions of books and periodicals, the situation had become intolerable.

△ △ △

In 1957 various groups including faculty, the board of trustees, and the administration began intensive studies of the library requirements of the University and particularly of the Homewood Campus. In his annual report for 1961, President Eisenhower summarized the planning for a great research library, which would hopefully meet the needs of the University until the year 2000. He stressed the centrality of the library's function. "It is," he said, "our citadel of knowledge, the physical and spiritual heart of the University." Although fund raising for a new library was admittedly a difficult endeavor, the president gave it priority over all other construction projects.

Work began on the library even before the required $4.7 million had been fully raised. By the fall of 1964 the new research library was open for business. Located at the east end of Keyser Quadrangle and overlooking the Bowl, the building is both handsome and thoroughly functional. Most all of the photographic, electronic, and acoustic appurtenances of modern scholarship have been incorporated, along with numerous individual studies and carrels, seminar and conference rooms. By 1967, only three years after it had opened, the library was serving at peak periods twenty thousand persons per week. The dream had finally been realized. In 1965 the trustees took an action which brought deep satisfaction to the University community. This magnificent new building was officially named the Milton S. Eisenhower Library.

The Eisenhower Library had been planned as a research library primarily for the use of faculty and graduate students. Although undergraduates also used the new facility, particularly at the upperclass level, the decision was made to renovate Gilman Hall, providing an undergraduate library with some 20,000 volumes as well as adequate study facilities, including a spacious reading room. The classrooms and seminar rooms in Gilman were increased in number and better provision was made for such services as the bank, the post office, and the bookstore, which had traditionally been housed in this building. Another welcome addition which was completed in this period was a new classroom building, Shaffer Hall, located on Wyman Quadrangle, and named for G. Wilson Shaffer, distinguished psychologist and for many years dean of Homewood Schools.

△ △ △

Finally, it should be noted that during the Eisenhower years, the physical welfare of the students and faculty at Homewood was hugely benefited through generous gifts in honor of a devoted friend of Johns Hopkins, the late Captain Newton H. White, Jr. The White Athletic Center, completed in 1965, has made possible a wide variety of indoor recreational activities, including a competition-sized swimming pool, numerous basketball, volleyball, badminton, squash, and handball courts, a wrestling room, a fencing room, and a weight training-exercise room. The Center has given a great boost to the Hopkins athletic program, which, while providing full opportunity for competition in intercollegiate sports, also emphasizes intramural competition and individual physical development.

△ △ △

The youngest and smallest of the major divisions of Johns Hopkins also profited substantially from the great building program of the Eisenhower decade. The significance of the School of Advanced International Studies was clearly recognized in 1960 when substantial financial support was made available by six leading foundations. This support made possible the construction of a new building on Massachusetts Avenue in Washington, D.C., completed in 1963, where the important instructional and research work of the School could go forward in an atmosphere of academic taste and efficiency. It is also noteworthy that at this time a ten-year grant of $30,000 per year from the Ford Foundation made possible a considerable expansion of the School's doctoral program. In Italy, the Bologna Center of the School moved into a new building in the spring of 1961. Made possible by a grant of Public Law 480 funds, the generosity of leading citizens of Bologna, and the untiring efforts of its founder and long-time director, Professor C. Grove Haines, this building now houses one of the finest collections of American source materials in Europe and is a focal point for European students who desire to undertake serious studies of American civilization as well as for American students who have a special interest in European studies.

Balanced budgets, strong government and private financial support, and a vast improvement in the physical plant were all essential in providing sinews of strength which had been sadly lacking for many years. Nonetheless, it is a mere commonplace to observe that such things in and of themselves by no means guarantee excellence in an institution such as a university. The lifeblood of Johns Hopkins has always been teaching and research, and the need for leadership in the academic area when Dr. Eisenhower assumed the presidency was strongly felt throughout the University community. The tenures of his two immediate predecessors had been short. A lack of coherence and a sense of drift in academic matters had begun to pervade the institution.

In his inaugural address as president of Johns Hopkins, Daniel Coit Gilman had remarked: "The truth is that most institutions are not free to build anew; they can only readjust." Gilman well understood the unique opportunity he had been given to build a great University without the constraints imposed by tradition and settled habits of mind. The problem faced by Johns Hopkins during the Eisenhower years was perhaps greater than that faced by Gilman to the extent that resuscitation may be more difficult than creation.

An adequate history of academic development at Johns Hopkins in the years 1957–67 would require far more space than is available in this brief history. The most important developments will be treated with some attempt to put them in a philosophical perspective.

In a summary account of the Eisenhower decade written in 1967, Mr. Charles S. Garland, chairman of the University Board of Trustees, argued that the word which most accurately characterized this period was *cohesion*. To get at Mr. Garland's meaning, it is useful to look at Dr. Eisenhower's concept of the basic function of the University as expressed in his annual report for 1961, entitled "Symbol for an Age":

> Of all human institutions the university has for centuries been the one most intimately concerned with the necessary accommodations between unity and multiplicity. Its contributions to multiplicity cannot be denied. In every century since the middle ages Western man has looked to the universities not simply as repositories of ancient wisdom but also as crucibles where by some mysterious alchemy the store of knowledge is constantly increased. . . .
>
> Though largely responsible for multiplicity, the free university has traditionally committed itself to the search for unity—to the unceasing though sometimes unsuccessful effort to bring philosophical order out of fragmented chaos. My dictionary tells me that the very word university is taken from two Latin words which mean "turned into one" or "combined into one whole." I do not want to grasp at straws, but will nonetheless accept this etymological evidence that a university is necessarily concerned with unity. . . .
>
> On this basis I find myself prepared to accept the free university as a valid symbol for our time. The university has become the focal point both for the staggering multiplicity growing out of the current "knowledge explosion" and also for efforts to achieve such unity of thought and purpose as will enable us to use this knowledge for human betterment rather than human destruction. What better symbol for a

time when all our hopes are expressed in what our free universities are trying to do?

In dealing with the centrifugal forces of multiplicity for which he rightly saw universities as largely responsible, Dr. Eisenhower constantly sought principles and means by which the essential unifying purpose of an institution such as Johns Hopkins could be achieved. This was a virtually superhuman task given not only the hundreds of academic specialties and sub-specialties but also the fact that Johns Hopkins was geographically divided into three main campuses, not to mention satellite operations such as the Bologna Center, and virtually independent research institutions such as the Applied Physics Laboratory.

It should not be implied that the movement toward greater unity and cohesion was some kind of a one-man operation directed from the president's office. The truth seems to be that forces impinging upon the various schools and divisions were tending in this direction from the mid-1950's. At every stage of the process, Dr. Eisenhower was supported by able and dedicated men such as Executive Vice-President P. Stewart Macaulay, Dean Thomas B. Turner of the School of Medicine, Dean Ernest L. Stebbins of the School of Hygiene and Public Health, G. Heberton Evans, Dean of the Faculty of Philosophy, G. Wilson Shaffer, Dean of the Homewood Schools, Dean Robert H. Roy of the School of Engineering Science, Dean Richard A. Mumma of the Evening College, Francis O. Wilcox, Dean of the School of Advanced International Studies, and Ralph E. Gibson, Director of the Applied Physics Laboratory. The significant fact was that the need for greater cohesion was understood at the decision-making level. It was an idea whose time had come.

△ △ △

The evidence for this major theme of the Eisenhower years is very strong and needs to be considered in some detail. A good place to begin is with a consideration of developments in the field of engineering.

In the first half of the twentieth century few fields of knowl-

Johns Hopkins, 1795–1873.

This 1901 photograph was taken in the Lanier Room of the University Library. From left to right: Basil L. Gildersleeve, Henry Rowland, Daniel Coit Gilman, William H. Welch, and Ira Remsen.

The famous Four Doctors oil painting. From left to right: Dr. Welch, Dr. Halsted, Dr. Osler, and Dr. Kelly.

Teaching laboratory in the New Hunterian Laboratory in east Baltimore, circa 1916.

Biology building on the corner of Eutaw and Little Ross Streets, circa 1900.

The Homewood Campus, circa 1920. Shown are Gilman Hall built in 1915; Maryland Hall, 1917; Latrobe Hall, 1916; and the power plant.

Medical Campus in east Baltimore in the 1920's. Broadway is on the extreme right.

edge had been more profoundly affected by the knowledge explosion than engineering. Specialties and sub-specialties had multiplied at a fantastic rate. The trend in most schools had been toward an ever-increasing number of vocationally oriented "how to" courses. As early as 1951, the Johns Hopkins School of Engineering set out to reverse this trend by dropping a number of specialized and practical courses and instead placing more emphasis upon basic courses in sciences and mathematics fundamental to all branches of engineering. In 1961 the process of integration was carried several steps further. To emphasize a concern with basic principles of engineering rather than technical training, the School was renamed the School of Engineering Science. At the same time, the Departments of Aeronautics, Civil Engineering, and Mechanical Engineering were combined into a single Department of Mechanics. It is useful to note that this action was taken after much study had indicated that topics in the broad field of mechanics could not be treated adequately within the confines of narrow departmental structures.

The final integrative stage was reached in 1966. For half a century the Faculties of Engineering and Philosophy at Homewood had been separate entities. It had become ever more apparent, however, that there was little philosophical justification for this separation. Undergraduate and graduate work in engineering at Johns Hopkins differed no more from work in the physical sciences than, for instance, the study of physics differed from the study of history. Accordingly, after much thought and study by Dean Roy and the engineering faculty, the School of Engineering Sciences merged with the Faculty of Philosophy to create a single new Faculty of Arts and Sciences. Since this merger, the continuing integration of disciplines unified by basic principles of investigation is evidenced by the creation of such departments as Earth and Planetary Sciences, Geography and Environmental Engineering, and Biomedical Engineering.

In his 1961 report, Dr. Eisenhower took note of the growing problem of the "two cultures" of the scientists and the humanists, a problem which had been powerfully stated by Sir Charles Snow in his Rede lecture at Cambridge University in 1959. Because of its traditional commitment to excellence in both of these broad areas, and because in the Hopkins environment the dynamic, vigorous, and essentially optimistic world of the scientists did seem increasingly to diverge from the less dynamic, less optimistic, but more value-oriented world of the humanists, Dr. Eisenhower was correct in stating that "Between these two worlds there exists tension, lack of sympathy, and a vast amount of misunderstanding."

To bridge this gap, to make meaningful synthesis more possible, the president proposed "the development of a . . . sphere of activity devoted to the history and philosophy of the natural sciences." In the same year that these words were written a generous friend of the University endowed a chair, and Dr. Harry Woolf became the Willis K. Shephard Professor of the History of Science. At first a part of the Department of History, in 1964 the Department of the History of Science was created as an independent entity. It has sought, primarily at the graduate level but with increasing attention to undergraduates, to elicit concepts by which the "two cultures" may move toward mutual understanding and appreciation of their vital connection.

Two new departments established at Homewood in the Eisenhower years provide further evidence of the way in which the University was moving away from traditional compartmentalization and toward integration. Sociology is a discipline which has developed and utilized its own concepts and which borrows liberally from many areas of the sciences and the humanities. Because of its significant links with other areas of research and teaching, as well as its own inherent importance, the decision was made to establish the Department of Social Relations. The work done in this area at Johns Hopkins won national acclaim in the late 1960's with the publication of Professor James S. Coleman's landmark study of racial integration in the schools, *Equality of Educational Opportunity*.

With the increasing use of quantitative techniques in virtually all fields of research, statistics was another discipline in need of support. This was forthcoming in 1962 with the establishment of the Department of Statistics. In 1972, in an integrative move, the work of this department was absorbed in the new Department of Mathematical Sciences. Research in statistics at Homewood has particularly emphasized the interplay between scientific problems and statistical inference. There is a close relationship with the Department of Biostatistics at the School of Hygiene and Public Health, including joint appointments of faculty and joint seminars.

△ △ △

One of the best illustrations of the concern exhibited in these years for cohesion, balance, and unity can be drawn from the area of the humanities. Over the course of its history Johns Hopkins had achieved a well-deserved reputation for greatness in the medical, physical, and biological sciences. Despite the fact that the University also had a long tradition of excellence in the social sciences and the humanities, the fact was that private and governmental support in these areas was much more difficult to achieve. The resulting imbalance was most obvious in the humanities. Teaching and research in languages, literature, history, and philosophy had actually suffered in many instances from diversions of funds impelled by federal matching grant requirements. In his 1963 annual report Dr. Eisenhower stressed the inequities inherent in this situation, pointing out that "a university is not a university, and it cannot have an *ethos* . . . unless a strong humanistic tradition permeates the institution."

In 1964 the president called upon the humanities faculty to appraise the state of its programs and to determine the direction it wished to follow in the future. After two years of intensive self-analysis a plan emerged, and Dr. Eisenhower asked the trustees to assign highest priority to raising the sum of $4.5 million for its implementation.

One of the key features of the plan as it was carried out was the creation of a new Humanities Center designed to circumvent the fragmentation frequently imposed by departmental barriers by placing in the Center the responsibility for initiating and coordinating programs emphasizing the fundamental unity of humanistic studies. Interdisciplinary teaching and research is encouraged at every level, be it undergraduate, graduate, or postdoctoral. Several year-long seminars have been conducted in such broad areas as the Middle Ages, the Renaissance, and the Eighteenth Century. These have been enriched by the participation of Visiting Scholars from many different countries and with many different perspectives.

Since the departments of the humanities group were generally quite small, many important specialties had no adequate representation. Accordingly, twenty-two new faculty positions were authorized. The plan also called for the creation of twenty postdoctoral fellowships which would be awarded annually to superior young scholars who would be enabled to spend a year in research and writing in the Hopkins environment. Graduate enrollment in the humanities was expanded, and an almost revolutionary new program was constructed to shorten the period of time required to achieve the Ph.D. degree.

All of these developments added up to a new injection of vitality for humanistic studies at Johns Hopkins. They also exhibit to the highest degree the concern for balance, cohesion, and unity which was the mark of the Eisenhower decade.

△ △ △

In the Medical Institutions the same theme was evident. A truly extraordinary degree of cooperation and coordination was becoming manifest among the Schools of Medicine, Hygiene and Public Health, and The Johns Hopkins Hospital. The administrative instrument which largely effected this cohesion was the Medical Planning and Development Committee, recommended by the Bard Committee Report of 1949. This committee, the MPD as it is generally known, is made up of the president of the University as presiding officer, and the senior officers of the Medical Institutions. It reports to a joint committee of the trustees of the University and the Hospital. After a slow start in the 1950's, it achieved ever-increasing effectiveness in the 1960's, enabling the Medical Institutions to reduce massive complexity to a large degree of common purpose. At the same time administrative streamlining within the two Schools was working to achieve the same end. As Dean of the School of Medicine Thomas B. Turner put it in his book, *Accounting of a Stewardship*, dealing with the years 1957–1968: "Without belaboring the point and with some exaggerative alliteration, it can be said that the Medical School during the past ten years has moved gradually from a collection of friendly feudal fiefdoms to a federation of functionally non-fractionated groups."

A revised curiculum of medical education was intensively studied in 1957–58 and inaugurated in September, 1958. Its goals as stated by Dean Turner were "to accelerate the pace of medical education, to bring greater scientific content to the entire curriculum, and to effect an overdue accommodation between the sciences and the humanities as they relate to medical education." The problems in medical education were actually similar to those in engineering. Exponential increases in knowledge were resulting in ever-proliferating specialties. The answer of the Medical School was also essentially the same as that given over a period of years by the engineering faculty. In dealing with massive complexity, the curriculum must be made both more basic and more flexible. The objective was the education of scholars of medicine, not the production of medical technologists.

Acceleration of the medical curriculum was seen as a real need because the production of qualified doctors had become a process which could, from college through residency training, easily require twelve or thirteen years. Medical education had become such a time-consuming and expensive proposition that applications to the nation's medical schools had actually declined since 1957. To ameliorate this situation, the revised curriculum provided for the admission each year of about twenty-five exceptional applicants who had completed two or three years of undergraduate work. The first year of this program combined both liberal arts and basic medical components with provision upon successful completion for awarding of the A.B. degree. As students move into subsequent years of the program, it has been found that the time required for attainment of the M.D. degree can be reduced by one and sometimes two years. It should also be noted that in an effort to help alleviate the the nation's shortage of qualified doctors, the School of Medicine moved to increase enrollment by twenty percent, from approximately 300 to about 360.*

△ △ △

For some years it had seemed desirable that the curriculum of the School of Advanced International Studies in Washington

---

* By 1972 Medical School enrollment had expanded to 475 students in years I-V.

provide opportunities for a selected number of liberal arts students at Homewood. In 1964 a B.A.–M.A. program was inaugurated by SAIS and the Faculty of Arts and Sciences which permits a number of qualified undergraduates to spend three years on the Homewood Campus pursuing a basic liberal arts program, a summer of intensive work in Western Europe, and the last two years in graduate study at the School. The B.A. degree is awarded at the end of the fourth year and the M.A. degree at the end of the fifth. Not only did this program provide a sensible integration with the SAIS curriculum, but it also served to increase the quality of the undergraduate social sciences applicants at Homewood.

△ △ △

The concepts of cohesion, coordination, and unity, which formed the main theme of the Eisenhower years, were manifested sometimes in administrative arrangements, sometimes in spontaneous cooperation which developed between major divisions or within them, and sometimes in the permeative influence of the theme itself in the entire University community. Two final illustrations should serve to point up its pervasive effects. The Applied Physics Laboratory, located in Howard County and performing important research and development work for the United States Navy, had from its inception had little contact with the main campuses in Baltimore. In the 1960's this pattern began to be broken as cooperative relationships began to develop. Particularly significant was the collaboration which developed between the Laboratory, the School of Medicine, and the engineering faculty at Homewood in the field of biomedical engineering. There were also fruitful joint projects between the APL and the School of Medicine in the fields of radiology and ophthalmology. The strong pervading attraction of unifying ideas is pointed up by the introduction of a Master of Liberal Arts program in the Evening College. For years Johns Hopkins had maintained an enviable reputation for research and teaching in the history of ideas, a field which was long the domain of the late great Professor Arthur O. Lovejoy. In 1963 it was decided that the new Master of Liberal Arts program would provide education for evening students who simply wanted to broaden their intellectual horizons through studies in the history of ideas. The program has been a great success, attracting exceptional students from a great diversity of occupations, and serving as a model for similar programs in other universities throughout the country.

An understanding of the theme of cohesion and unity makes possible a comprehension of how the University sought in these years to deal with the fragmenting forces of multiplicity and growth. It is obviously not possible to treat all significant developments of the Eisenhower era under this rubric. Nor is it possible in a brief history to mention more than a very few of the hundreds of examples of progress in scores of different areas which would all add up to a complex portrait of a great institution in the business of fulfilling its social contract with humanity. In this connection the theme of "outreach"—of increasing involvement with crucial human problems—was becoming more insistent from the mid-sixties onward. The pressures from the outside world were sometimes threatening to the hard-won spirit of cohesion, but they could not be ignored.

△ △ △

The Medical Institutions had, of course, always been involved with the most profound of human problems, but as Dean Turner has testified, the most significant development at the School of Medicine in the ten years from 1957 to 1967 was "a gradually dawning understanding of the role of the Medical Institutions as a social instrument with deep obligation to the medical profession on the one hand and to society in general on the other . . ."

In the sixties the School of Medicine launched a broad-scale attack on the diseases affecting children. A fourteen-story, $14 million Children's Medical and Surgical Center was opened in 1964. The Center provided facilities for some of the most advanced work in the world in the field of pediatrics, including a very substantial addition to the capacity of the Hospital. This commitment to the welfare of children was reinforced a few years later with the completion of a building housing the John F. Kennedy Institute for Habilitation of the Mentally and Physically Handicapped Child. Although administratively a separate entity, the Institute is staffed by the School of Medicine and the closest kind of relationship exists. Patient care, patient education, clinical training, and research are all emphasized. Treatment is offered for diseases such as cerebral palsy, where specialized care in the past has been practically non-existent. These developments point up the fact that the Medical Institutions have massively extended their outreach to children throughout the world.

Other types of deep involvement with social problems can be cited. The ongoing efforts of the School of Hygiene and Public Health in raising health standards in scores of different countries were highlighted in 1961 with the establishment of the Department of International Health. The creation of this unit made possible a whole series of long-term research and training activities in Asia, Africa, and Latin America. Also in the early sixties there were created in the School the Departments of Population Dynamics and Medical Care and Hospitals. Research and teaching in the area of population dynamics were very controversial at this time, but in subsequent years, this vital area has been supported by multi-million-dollar grants from both private foundations and government. The Department of Medical Care and Hospitals was established to deal with one of the greatest of contemporary problems in this and other countries—the provision of adequate systems of health and medical care services. In its efforts the Department has utilized the most advanced concepts of operations research and systems analysis and has carried out a number of comparative studies of health care systems in the United States and in other countries. Also in the sixties the School of Medicine inaugurated cooperative relationships with medical schools at the American University in Beirut, the University of Ibadan in Nigeria, and the Cayetano Heredia University in Lima, Peru, involving faculty exchanges designed to raise the level of medical education in the third world. Closer to home, the School of Medicine continued to provide a vast array of free or low-cost medical services for the population of east Baltimore and also began consideration of a proposal to provide complete prepaid medical care to the residents of Columbia, a new town located in Howard County between Baltimore and Washington.

△ △ △

At the School of Advanced International Studies the involvement was different but no less significant. The Washington Center of Foreign Policy Research was founded in 1957 to carry forward intensive studies in the general area of international relations and more specifically in problems of American foreign policy. The Center maintains a certain independence in the School, but the connection is nonetheless close since permanent members of the Center also hold joint appointments as faculty members of SAIS. The Center has been supported by grants from foundations and the federal government. Roundtable discussions are frequently held with visiting officials, journalists, and scholars leading to fruitful exchanges of views. Many affiliates of the Center have held appointments at the highest levels of government, and no one familiar with the Washington scene would dispute its impressive influence. Another important activity sponsored by the School has been the Conferences of Corporate Executives. Some four or five of these conferences are held each year for executives representing hundreds of organizations with interests abroad. Usually specializing in a given geographic area of the world such as Latin America or a country such as Egypt, the Conferences bring together top government officials, academicians, and business executives for in-depth discussions of developing conditions and attitudes. The public service activities of the School also increased substantially in these years with many special seminars and conferences being held for members of Congress, Foreign Service Officers, and young diplomats from Asia, Africa, and Latin America.

△ △ △

Faculty, students, and alumni are constituencies of vital importance to any university and cannot be neglected here. The overall faculty of the various schools and divisions of the University increased by several hundred in the decade 1957–67. No process is more vital to the welfare of Johns Hopkins than the recruitment of outstanding scholars and scientists to fill new and old positions. Thousands of hours were spent by innumerable committees in search of individuals who could meet the highest standards not only of professional competence but of creativeness as well. That these efforts were successful is evidenced by the scores of Hopkins faculty included in the ranks of the National Academy of Sciences, the American Academy of Arts and Sciences, and American Men of Science. Continuing excellence at the highest faculty level received added assurance during this period through the creation of thirteen endowed chairs, eight at the Medical Institutions, three at Homewood, and two at SAIS.

The number of undergraduates at Homewood increased by 460 during this period to a total of 1,768 in 1966–67, and their academic quality as measured by standard indices improved greatly. Median scores on the college board examinations had not been impressive in 1956, but ten years later they indicated that Hopkins was attracting its entering students from the top 2 percent of all secondary school graduates. Also the retention rate among undergraduates rose in these years from 69 to 83 percent. Dr. Eisenhower placed great emphasis upon raising the quality of academic and extracurricular student life. Much effort went into building greater flexibility into academic programs and into providing facilities and services for undergraduates including the appointment of an associate dean for undergraduate studies, a director of undergraduate student affairs, a financial aid officer, and additional dormitory counselors.

The Eisenhower decade witnessed a sharp increase in the number of graduate students. It has been noted that enrollment rose by 20 percent in the School of Medicine. In the School of Hygiene and Public Health the number of students rose from 156 in 1956–57 to 320 in 1967–68. The School of Advanced International Studies nearly quadrupled its enrollment from 76 in 1956–57 to 287 in 1966–67. The number of Ph.D. candidates in the arts and sciences departments at Homewood increased by nearly 100 percent, from approximately 700 in 1956–57 to 1,370 ten years later. This huge expansion in graduate enrollment was largely made possible by government and private support for a varied array of educational and research programs. Such support also accounted for a dramatic increase in the number of postdoctoral students. In 1956–57 there were about 300 of these highly trained individuals in residence at the University. In 1966–67 there were more than 800. While most postdoctorals were associated with the Medical Institutions, there were an increasing number attached to the Faculty of Arts and Sciences. In relation to total enrollment Johns Hopkins had a higher proportion of postdoctoral students than any other American university. This was education to a higher power, closely related to the massive knowledge explosion of the post-World War II era. Dr. Eisenhower saw this development as so important as "to constitute virtually a new dimension in education."

The Evening College (formerly McCoy College) continued to enroll both undergraduate and graduate students in a wide variety of programs in the liberal arts, business administration, and engineering. Registrations increased substantially and the number of credit courses offered grew from 207 to 264. The quality of the instruction was significantly strengthened. Several new master's programs were inaugurated, including the Master of Liberal Arts discussed above. It is noteworthy that the percentage of college graduates in the student body rose from 30 to 38 percent.

Dr. Eisenhower well understood the crucial importance of a loyal alumni constituency. Foundations and corporations could hardly be expected to provide support to the University unless the alumni did their part. Strenuous and successful efforts were made in these years to revitalize the existing alumni clubs and to create additional organizations providing a base for support in virtually every major population center in the country. Dr. Eisenhower made it a practice to visit a number of these clubs each year, as did a number of faculty and administrators. The movement toward creation of a strong and effective alumni body was also aided immeasurably by the untiring efforts of Osmar P. Steinwald, long-time Director of Alumni Relations. The tangible evidence of success in this area is perhaps best evidenced by the increase in alumni giving to the University from $166,000 in 1956 to more than $600,000 in 1967. One of the means through which the very diverse Hopkins alumni constituency was brought closer together was through the agency of the *Johns Hopkins Magazine*. Founded in the early 1950's and stamped with a unique character by its first editor, Corbin Gwaltney, the *Magazine* continued in the Eisenhower years under the editorship of Ronald Wolk and Anthony Neville to garner prizes for distinction in almost every category.

In September of 1966, Dr. Eisenhower was sixty-seven years of age. For forty years he had held positions of great responsibility in government and higher education. A decade of splendid leadership fueled by untiring effort had taken its toll. He felt that the time for retirement had come and requested that the trustees select a successor and relieve him of his duties by June 30, 1967.

The selection committee of the Board of Trustees was well aware of its crucial responsibility. Over a period of seven months it was aided in its deliberations by the advice and counsel of a twenty-one member faculty and deans committee and by consultation with many persons expert in the problems of higher education. One hundred fifty candidates were screened and a number were personally interviewed. The choice finally settled on Dr. Lincoln Gordon, who, at the age of 53, became the ninth president of The Johns Hopkins University.

Like his predecessor, Dr. Gordon brought to his new post a wealth of experience in government and higher education. A Harvard graduate and a Rhodes Scholar, Dr. Gordon had been awarded the Doctor of Philosophy degree from Oxford in recognition of his book, *The Public Corporation in Great Britain*. A political economist, he had held faculty positions at Harvard, including a prestigious chair. There had been frequent intervals of public service such as participation in the Marshall Plan and the Alliance for Progress. From 1961 to 1966 he served as Ambassador to Brazil, and at the time of his selection as president of Johns Hopkins, he held the position of Assistant Secretary of State for Inter-American Affairs.

President Gordon assumed the burdens of office on July 1, 1967. In the traditional inaugural address delivered on February 22, 1968, he emphasized the vast changes which had taken place in higher education since the retirement of Daniel Coit Gilman in 1902. Whereas Johns Hopkins had in its early years been small and preeminent in a society where higher education was a luxury enjoyed by a very few in a few very select institutions, the University still proudly maintained its tradition of excellence but existed in an environment where millions looked upon higher education as almost a natural right and where giant multiversities dotted the landscape from Maine to California. In President Remsen's first budget, 88 percent of income came from endowment and tuition. In Dr. Eisenhower's last budget only 23 percent came from these sources, and no less than 53 percent derived from federal government support. The problems presented by these sobering facts were obvious, but the solutions could not be found by abandoning the traditions of smallness, independence, and excellence that had served the University so well since 1876. Dr. Gordon found continuing relevance for the ideals of Johns Hopkins:

> Whatever the future may now bring, we can say with confidence, short of an all-destroying nuclear holocaust, that it will desperately need the qualities we here seek to foster: intellectual curiosity and discipline; intelligence trained at the frontiers of unfolding knowledge but infused with humanity; dedication combined with objectivity; operational idealism; the search for truth, not only for its own sake but because in the words adopted as our motto, 'the truth shall make you free.'

The Gordon administration had a duration of about four years—from July, 1967 to March, 1971. These were years of great stress in American society and the pressures generated seemed frequently to focus upon the nation's colleges and universities. This was most apparent in the case of the developing opposition to the war in Vietnam, but the overall forces involved were quite diverse. The aspirations of women and blacks, the involvement of universities with military research projects and R.O.T.C., the questions of governance and student rights were all problems which burst suddenly upon many of the most prestigious campuses in the late 1960's. Johns Hopkins was not a major cauldron of this seething discontent which boiled over in such institutions as Cornell, Columbia, Stanford, and the University of California. It was probably insulated to a large extent by its large enrollment of graduate students whose interests tended, in most cases, though not all, to be more professional than political. Nonetheless, Hopkins was hardly unaffected by these currents. There were those times when tempers flared and rational discussion seemed to be at a discount. Confrontations and consultations with activist groups were a major item on President Gordon's agenda. Added to these problems was a financial crisis in the University the likes of which had not been experienced since the years of the Great Depression.

In these years of discontent the focus of headline-making activity was at Homewood, site of the undergraduate program. Highly significant developments were taking place in other schools and divisions of the University, but the dramatic action was, ostensibly at least, on the North Baltimore campus. The *Johns Hopkins Magazine* mirrored the shift in emphasis that had occurred. In the spring of 1967 it had devoted an entire issue to the Renaissance. In April, 1970 the articles dealt with the problem of the University's relationship with the Applied Physics Laboratory, with the plight of women faculty members, with the results of school desegregation, and a comparison of past and contemporary student and faculty attitudes and opinions by Dean Emeritus G. Wilson Shaffer. The age of relevance had indeed arrived.

The new discontents came slowly to the Hopkins scene. In December, 1967 the *Johns Hopkins Journal*, after a sampling of undergraduate opinion, reported: "Foreign policy, Vietnam, and the draft played a strictly secondary role in their thinking. Uppermost in their minds was the concern for getting along with people of all kinds and a concern for avoiding middle class standards and conformity at all costs."

Meanwhile campus unrest in the nation continued to spread. R.O.T.C. came under frequent attack, both verbal and violent. In the fall of 1967, the Academic Council, the decision-making body on matters of academic policy for the division of Arts and Sciences, voted to remove credit from all courses taught by the Army R.O.T.C. This decision was made entirely on academic grounds and was accepted by the Army.

In the spring of 1969, the calm which had pervaded Homewood, even at a time when other institutions were racked by tumult, was rudely shattered. The precipitant in the chain of events was a drug raid on campus on the night of April 24 in which three freshmen were arrested for possession of marijuana and amphetamines. The resulting protest of this police action rapidly expanded to include other issues, including the continuance of R.O.T.C. on campus as well as recruiting by the military, intelligence agencies of the government, and corporations producing "war and social control material for use at home and abroad." The events of late April and May included a number of meetings and confrontations with President Gordon and one unauthorized sit-in at Homewood House by about thirty students. In all of these actions the radical organization, Students for a Democratic Society or SDS, played a leading role.

△ △ △

In this yeasty environment of protest and confrontation President Gordon was conciliatory but firm on principle. On April 21, he had reported to the Board of Trustees on the subject of campus unrest: "The basic remedy must be to draw together the vast majority of students, faculty, administrators, and governing boards in a positive effort to recognize and respond to legitimate desires for reform, while devising new, prompt, and efficient means to cope with the intransigent disrupture. Neither of those is easy." At an open meeting of the University community in Keyser Quadrangle on May 16, the president strongly affirmed his belief in the free university in which all opinions have the right to compete for attention and in which the rights of both minorities and majorities are respected. He defended the presence of R.O.T.C. as a "wholly voluntary activity, no longer given academic credit," but of interest to a significant number of Hopkins students. Until he found evidence that it interfered with "the rights and freedoms of other members of the community," there was "a very strong presumption in favor of permitting the interested group of students to continue this activity." With respect to recruiting he was equally forthright in defending the rights of all members of the student community: "I see no reason why the disapproval of those agencies and institutions by another group of students should deprive the first group of the convenience of being interviewed on campus."

Three weeks later commencement exercises provided another forum for more decorous confrontation. On this occasion a student speaker dealt with the root issue of campus protest, the war in Vietnam. This was strongly deplored since it had "forced the United States to prostitute its legitimate priorities and utilize its resources to bomb cities and not to build them, to defoliate land and not to cultivate it, to slaughter children and not to feed them." The selective service system was denounced as well as the American university's alleged "support of the war through secret research fostering the development of increasingly efficient instruments of death." The principal speaker, President Kingman Brewster of Yale, condemned mob rule and the decline of rational discourse. He defended the pursuit of knowledge for its own sake, asserting: "I am against the anti-intellectual intellectual who would impose a test of relevance upon us all." President Gordon lamented the breakdown of the sense of community at all levels of society but particularly within the university, for "no community is more vulnerable to the forces of dissension than a university." So the spring of 1969 passed into history.

The vintage year for student protest in the nation and at Johns Hopkins was 1969–70. Vietnam Moratorium Day came early in the academic year. On October 15, students gathered early at Levering Hall to join in "leafletting the community." By noon a crowd of several hundred students gathered on Keyser Quadrangle for an afternoon teach-in featuring speeches from professors, students, area clergymen, and former U.S. Senator Ernest Gruening of Alaska. American involvement in Vietnam was roundly and routinely deplored. The Academic Council, meeting in Shriver Hall, was briefly besieged by a group of about fifty students, demanding that business be cancelled in the spirit of the day. About 4 P.M., the crowd, now swelled to about 3,000 students and sympathizers, marched down through Wyman Quadrangle, and for a moment it seemed that the Academic Council would suffer complete disruption of its meeting if not worse. The march righted itself however and with banners flying proceeded to a downtown rally. There they were joined by a 100-man contingent from the Medical Institutions who had participated in their own teach-in at Hurd Auditorium. Later in the evening a large crowd again gathered on Keyser Quadrangle for a candlelight memorial service to honor some eight Johns Hopkins alumni who had lost their lives in Vietnam. At SAIS in Washington a morning-long teach-in attracted some 150 participants. All in all this was the most impressive day of protest in the history of the University.

Despite pressure from students and many faculty members, President Gordon refused to suspend academic and administrative operations for the day of the Moratorium protest. In reply to a Student Council resolution that the University close on the 15th, Dr. Gordon stated that at Hopkins "there is no inhibition on individual or organized manifestations of opinion, so long as they do not impair freedom of others or interfere with the normal functioning of the University."

Throughout the academic year one issue after another competed for attention in the Homewood environment. There was legitimate concern that, as an intellectually elite institution, Johns Hopkins had neglected the needs and aspirations of minority groups, particularly in its recruiting of students. Although serious efforts to improve upon this situation had begun in the mid-sixties, it was still true that in 1969, 95.8 percent of University enrollment was white, with only 174 minority group students in the various divisions. With the encouragement of the administration, renewed efforts began to be made to improve upon this situation. The Black Graduate Students Association sent representatives to a number of primarily black colleges, telling the story of Johns Hopkins and seeking to interest qualified applicants. These efforts and those of administrators in the Medical Institutions and at SAIS bore some fruit, for by the fall of 1970, the percentage of minority students had risen to 5.8 or a total of about 239.

In March, 1970 the *Johns Hopkins Journal* reported the question of governance to be "the top issue on the Homewood campus this year." What the issue seemed to boil down to was whether undergraduate and graduate students were to be allowed to participate in some of the key decisions in the realm of academic affairs. The engine of participation was to be a University Senate with representation from various constituencies, including students. The Academic Council, long supreme in matters of curriculum and faculty appointments, tenure, and promotion, was none too enthusiastic about this proposal. Various investigative committees and an advisory council were appointed, but no real structural changes in academic governance have yet resulted. Nonetheless, in recent years student input has been incorporated in a number of important areas. Since 1971, a graduating senior has been elected each year to the board of trustees for a four-year term. Students from the various divisions also serve on the Public Interest Investment Advisory Committee which advises the trustees on the voting of the University's common stock holdings in cases involving shareholder proposals concerning ecological problems, employment practices, and the foreign policies of U.S. corporations. Students are intimately involved in the planning of the Centennial celebration and have a preponderant voice in the management of the Student Union.

In the spring of 1970, the remote and little understood Applied Physics Laboratory also surfaced as an issue at Homewood. As the *Johns Hopkins Magazine* put it: "A small group of students calling themselves the Committee on APL were arguing, before anyone who would listen, that society has too many pressing environmental and social problems needing solutions for Johns Hopkins to be harboring a $50 million-a-year partner in the military-industrial complex." At first student activists seemed to be calling for a separation of the University and the Laboratory. Later the Committee agreed that APL should remain a part of Hopkins but that it should be converted to "socially useful" activity. It also demanded that no new classified research projects be initiated and that all currently classified work being done at the Laboratory be terminated by the end of fiscal 1971. In a reply to the Committee on April 11, the president rejected most of the Committee's proposals but pointed out that the APL staff and the University's APL Advisory Board were both greatly interested "in expanding the work of APL in such fields as health, urban affairs, and transportation." The issue simmered down as students dispersed for the summer, but it is noteworthy that, on its own initiative, the Laboratory has greatly expanded its programs outside of the defense area in recent years with work being carried out for and in cooperation with the National Aeronautics and Space Administration, the National Institutes of Health, the Veterans Administration, the Department of Transportation, the Coast Guard, and the Medical Institutions of the University.

The year of discord ended appropriately. In late April 1970, student discontent over the issues of military recruiting on campus, APL, R.O.T.C., and governance reached a pinnacle. A student strike was called, and about half the undergraduates refused to attend classes. At the end of two days an accommodation was reached with the administration which ended the strike. Military recruiting on campus was to be suspended unless students voted in a referendum to retain it. The subsequent vote was close, but the opponents of recruiting won what was regarded as a victory over the military-university establishment.* In early May the Cambodian incursion and the shootings of students at Kent State produced a cresting wave of protest which rolled over the nation's campuses. Hopkins students participated in rallies in Washington and Baltimore. The General Faculty Assembly at Homewood resolved that classes should be suspended for a day, and the administration reflected the general sense of crisis in urging the faculty "to allow any student to take full advantage of the existing flexibilities in the completion of course requirements." President Gordon cosigned a letter of protest to President Nixon expressing alarm over "the dangers of an unprecedented alienation of America's youth." In keeping with his previously stated principles, however, there was no official closing of the University.

△ △ △

The tumult of these years should not obscure the fact that the work of the University went on. Change is the necessary ingredient of progress, and the Gordon years witnessed a number of changes of great importance. In the Shriver Hall meeting of October 15, 1969, which was briefly besieged by protesting students, the Academic Council recommended that female undergraduates be admitted for the 1970–71 school year. Subsequently, both the president and the board of trustees approved the idea of coeducation and the 93-year tradition of an all-

---

* The victory was short-lived, however, for military recruiting on campus was reinstated by the Board of Trustees in October, 1970.

male undergraduate enrollment was broken. No elaborate preparations were made to prepare for the influx of women. The attitude seemed to be that the necessary things would be done as they became apparent. Alumni resistance was decidedly minimal, and the feeling among faculty and students was strongly in favor, since segregation by sex seemed more anachronistic every year.

In the fall of 1970 ninety women were admitted to the Homewood undergraduate division. There were a few problems with housing, and some of the women complained of the lack of special counseling and other services. Most, however, seemed to adjust remarkably well to the University's ancient policy of providing all students with a maximum of freedom and independence. The *Magazine* reported, that, all in all, the presence of women undergraduates "made surprisingly few changes in campus life." The percentage of women in the undergraduate student body has continued to increase so that in 1973–74 there were 472 females in a total enrollment of 2,073.

△ △ △

No history of Johns Hopkins, however brief, would be complete without some treatment of lacrosse, a sport which has long aroused passion in the hearts of thousands of Hopkins students and graduates. Since the 1880's when the sport took root at the University, lacrosse has been in many ways to Johns Hopkins what football is to Notre Dame and basketball is to U.C.L.A. There is a difference, however, in that lacrosse has never been commercialized at Homewood and retains a distinct amateur flavor. The sport has perhaps been fortunate in that it has not yet attracted the corrupting embrace of the mass media. It has remained a game for athletes and *aficionados,* many of whom reside in the Baltimore area. In recent years, an increasing number of colleges and universities have fielded teams and mounted intensive player-recruitment campaigns. Although Hopkins offers no lacrosse scholarships and all athletes must measure up to tough academic standards, the University continues to attract talented players whose ambition is to become part of a long and glorious tradition.

Since 1888, when Hopkins was represented by its first official team, the Blue Jays through 1974 have won or shared 30 national championships. There have been 61 winning seasons, only 15 losing ones, and 11 with ties. For 27 collegiate seasons the Blue Jays have been unbeaten, and in 26 there was only one loss. Since 1922 when the team was first selected, Hopkins has produced 104 All-American players and has contributed 26 of the 108 members of the Lacrosse Hall of Fame, which is appropriately located in the Newton H. White, Jr. Athletic Center at Homewood. Johns Hopkins has represented the United States in the only Olympic Games in which the sport was played, tying for first place in 1928 and finishing alone in first in 1932. Although the late 1960's were frequently years of crisis and confrontation on campus, the lacrosse situation left little to be desired, with Coach Bob Scott's Blue Jays winning or sharing national championships in 1967, 1968, and 1969. Even though other sports must usually take a back seat to lacrosse at Homewood, it is noteworthy that for the same three years, the Hopkins football team either won or shared the Middle Atlantic Conference Southern Division title, and that a truly superb swimming team won five conference championships from 1969 through 1974.

△ △ △

Examples of the University's growing commitment to "outreach" were the establishment of a Center for Urban Affairs in December, 1968, and the Greater Homewood Community Corporation in May, 1969. Supported by grants from the Ford Foundation and government and private sources, the Center was designed to carry out extensive research and educational training in urban problems. Not a degree-granting division of the University, the Center would act as a catalyst in bringing together expertise in urban affairs which already existed in the various schools and divisions. The headquarters of the Center was originally established at the campus of the Medical Institutions, but was moved in the summer of 1972 to Homewood, where it has been renamed the Center for Metropolitan Planning and Research. An intensive effort has been made to relate the new Center's programs closely to the overall pattern of the

University's teaching and research. Particularly significant have been new fellowship programs. Two of these enable undergraduates in various Homewood departments to serve as interns either in Baltimore municipal departments or in the offices of elected officials. Another program, the Foreign Fellowship Program, makes it possible for European scholars and students of urban problems to come to the Center for a period of research and learning activity in which the problems of their cities can be viewed from the perspective of the American environment.

The Greater Homewood Community Corporation was the result of an initiative taken by the University in 1967. With support provided for two years by Title I of the Higher Education Act of 1965 and University matching funds, the original project set out to identify and document neighborhood issues and develop local leadership and resources to deal with those issues in a 3½-square-mile area surrounding the Homewood Campus. Today the Corporation is involved in a variety of community improvement activities which demonstrate to the 40,000 people who reside in this area that Johns Hopkins is something more than a remote and uncaring ivory tower. Johns Hopkins is a partner in this effort, working closely with the Corporation through its Office of Community Affairs and through membership on the Corporation's Board of Directors.

In other developments at Homewood during these years, ground was broken late in 1968 for a new administration building, located immediately to the south of Levering Hall. Occupied in the summer of 1971, the building was named Garland Hall in honor of Charles S. Garland, long-time dedicated and distinguished chairman of the board of trustees. Today it houses the offices of the president of the University, the provost, the vice-presidents, and various offices of the central administration as well as some administrative offices of the Arts and Sciences division. This building was the first structure on the campus (with the possible exception of the Eisenhower Library) to depart substantially from the Georgian tradition set by Homewood House. In the spring of 1969, a new Alumni House at 3211 North Charles Street opened its doors. The gift of Jacob Hain, this building was subsequently named the Steinwald Alumni House in honor of Osmar P. Steinwald, the University's first director of Alumni Relations. The attractive residence now houses the staffs of the Alumni Relations and Annual Giving offices, and serves as headquarters for the Alumni Association and its thirty-six branches scattered throughout the country.

In a brief treatment such as this, little attention has been or can be given to the extraordinary quantity and quality of the research and development activities which characterize every division of the University in the second half of the twentieth century. A full telling of this story would require more volumes than most writers or readers would care to contemplate. The preceding pages have pictured the University's reactions to a period of stress. To demonstrate that the crisis atmosphere so prevalent in these years had little or no effect upon the great ongoing mission of Johns Hopkins, it would seem useful, despite the necessity for brevity, to provide some information on the scope of research and development efforts in the years 1966-1970. The focus will be on the Medical Institutions.

Late in 1966, the *Johns Hopkins Journal* reported that Hopkins engineers and physicians were "developing mechanical hearts, designing ultrasonic instruments for eye and brain surgery, relieving overworked hearts by applying principles of fluid dynamics, using telemetry and computers to monitor patients and sewing transparent windows into abdominal walls to observe physiological changes in the stomach." Early in 1967 it was announced that medical researchers were studying the relation of emotional stress to dwarfism, pioneering a new technique called electrodermal audiometry designed to extract hearing-related information from deaf babies and children, and automating the screening process for detecting uterine cancer. In the fall, the Department of Psychiatry received an $825,000 grant from the National Institute of Mental Health to train personnel in the field of suicide prevention. Late in the year it was reported that Haldan K. Hartline, former chairman of the

Department of Biophysics, would share the 1967 Nobel prize in medicine for work on the primary chemical and physiological processes in the eye.

In 1968, the Rockefeller Foundation provided support for a School of Hygiene study of schistosomiasis or "snail fever," a disease which afflicts 150 million people throughout the world. In the School of Medicine a major study of hypertension and its relation to kidney disease was announced.

It was reported in February, 1969, that Hopkins medical scientists were searching for solutions to the mysteries surrounding the body's immunologic or built-in defense system through a study of the complexities of the mammalian womb. A wide-ranging probe of the problems of human nutrition was announced by the Department of International Health of the School of Hygiene. An Office of Health Care Programs was established to deal with outpatient services in east Baltimore as well as the developing prepaid comprehensive care system in the new city of Columbia, Maryland.

In the summer of 1969, the public was informed that The Johns Hopkins Hospital had been selected by the World Health Organization as the only American hospital to participate in a global study of breast cancer. At the same time intensive studies of treatment methods for narcotics addiction and disorders producing mental retardation were noted in the press. In September, the *Johns Hopkins Journal* reported on a long-awaited study of the effects of "the pill" made by a team headed by Dr. Philip E. Sartwell of the School of Hygiene and Public Health. A new unit was established in the Children's Medical and Surgical Center to identify mental problems of children and young teenagers. Late in the year the new Department of Neurology of the medical school received a substantial grant from the Hartford Foundation to study degenerative diseases of the nervous system such as multiple sclerosis and cerebral palsy.

Early in 1970, new studies were announced of the behavioral effects of hallucinogenic drugs and of ways to build resistance to hay fever. Hopkins surgeons became the first in the United States to provide artificial hip replacements. Dr. Vincent L. Gott, one of the doctors who had performed Johns Hopkins' first and only heart transplant operation in 1968, noted that the survival period for such operations averaged only two or three months and that his team intended to concentrate on the development of several mechanical systems designed to sustain damaged hearts. In the fall, the School of Hygiene reported a study designed to control the destructive habits of bats through an understanding of the high-frequency sounds produced in locating each other, and also how a mother bat can identify her babies in the dark amid a clamor of calls from many bats. William B. Kouwenhoven, former dean of the School of Engineering and lecturer in surgery at the School of Medicine since 1956, was honored in 1970 by the Institute of Electrical and Electronics Engineers for his work in developing the basis and practical means of defibrillating the heart externally and the technique of closed chest cardiac massage. In 1973, Dr. Kouwenhoven, at the age of 87, received the Albert Lasker Clinical Medical Research Award for what the Lasker Foundation jury termed his "landmark contributions to the care of cardiac patients."

Late in 1970, the results of a five-year collaborative effort involving the Applied Physics Laboratory, the School of Medicine and the School of Hygiene and Public Health were presented to a gathering of several hundred physicians, researchers, and press representatives. Among the presentations were a new artificial limb system for the upper extremities operated by a combined action of shoulder and back muscles with an electrically powered system, a left-heart bypass pump which stimulates the pulsatile pattern of blood flow, a method of employing an argon laser beam to seal blood vessels and stop hemorrhaging within the eye, and the use of fluorescein, a fluorescing dye, for diagnosing disorders in the retinal vascular system.

The developments outlined above occurred in a period of little more than four years and are confined to the Medical Institutions. Even so, the treatment is by no means exhaustive, and represents only a fraction of the total ongoing research and development effort. It hopefully provides the reader with some idea of the vital importance and staggering complexity of the work that goes on in one of the great medical research centers of the world.

Two significant additions to the Medical Institutions were completed in 1968, after several years of planning and construction. On September 18, the Ernest Lyman Stebbins Building of the School of Hygiene and Public Health was dedicated. Named for the long-time dean of the School, the ten-story structure contains student seminar rooms, individual student carrels, a large student study area, teaching table laboratories, libraries, faculty offices, departmental seminar and conference rooms, and a ninth floor cafeteria that serves the entire School. The new building was part of a development program, which since 1961, had enabled the School to more than double its physical size and student enrollment.

On December 6, 1968, another distinguished dean emeritus was honored when the School of Medicine dedicated the Thomas B. Turner Auditorium. This building houses a 750-seat auditorium, four large seminar rooms, a 150-seat auditorium, the School's computer center, and a number of administrative offices. The auditoriums and seminar rooms are used for teaching medical students, for the continuing education of physicians, and for meetings and programs sponsored by medical and health-related groups.

At the School of Advanced International Studies there were also important developments during the years of Lincoln Gordon's presidency. In the spring of 1968, it was announced that the Washington Center of Foreign Policy Research had received a $345,000 Ford Foundation grant to study basic national and international developments affecting American foreign policy. In 1969, the Center for Canadian Studies was established. Funded by the William H. Donner Foundation and the Donner Canadian Foundation, with a $1 million grant, the new Center became the first such enterprise in the nation to operate at the graduate level. In October, 1970, the School celebrated its twenty-fifth anniversary in a ceremony attended by many dignitaries and featuring an address by former Secretary of State Dean Acheson.

It is perhaps ironic that modern private universities find it easier to withstand the strains of confrontation, turmoil, and ideological division than to struggle with serious financial crises. Despite inevitable inertia, they are in truth well adapted to deal with the former situation, since historically, they have functioned as one of society's most important crucibles where conflicting claims and opinions are argued and sometimes resolved. Financial anemia, however, is a disease which affects a university's vitals. It can weaken an institution's morale as the atmosphere begins to be dominated by feelings of doubt and uncertainty.

In the years 1969–71, steadily increasing deficits at Johns Hopkins eventuated in the greatest financial crisis since the 1930's. In fiscal 1969, the deficit was a modest but ominous $530,000. In 1970, it was an alarming $2.9 million. By 1971, it was a staggering $4.2 million. While the seriousness of the situation had become readily apparent, its causes admitted then and now of no simple explanation. A high rate of inflation was one important factor, contributing to a persistent rise in costs for goods and services. Under-recovery of indirect costs for sponsored research resulting from ever-changing and complex accounting and auditing requirements imposed by the federal government was another significant element, as was the sharp downturn in federal support of graduate education and research in the basic and applied sciences.

A rapid rise in the size of the Arts and Sciences faculty and a near doubling of administrative personnel in the University generally had a crucial causative impact on the developing crisis. This expansion was to some extent affected by the deliberations of a long-range planning commission appointed by President Eisenhower in 1964. At this time the University's financial condition was one of rosy good health and featured substantial yearly surpluses of revenues over expenditures. After more than 100 meetings over a two-year period, the committee's report was submitted in June, 1966. Among the recommendations made were an increase of 140 in the Faculty of Arts and Sciences without a proportionate increase in student enrollment, as well as an expansion of the University administration to cope with the ever-growing complexity of higher education.

Although these recommendations were never officially endorsed by the faculty, the trustees, or President Eisenhower, they had a considerable effect upon the policies of the Gordon administration. With the benefit of hindsight, it can perhaps be said that the financial crisis of 1969–71 was largely the result of the fact that these recommendations continued to be implemented even when it was clear that the necessary resources did not exist. Seventy positions were added to the faculty of Arts and Sciences while the total enrollment of graduate and undergraduate students at Homewood increased by only about one hundred. From 1966 to 1971, the number of administrative personnel nearly doubled from 150 to 297.* Reflecting this expansion total University expenditures for instruction, departmental research, and administration from fiscal 1967 through fiscal 1971 rose by nearly $11 million. Income from tuition and fees, endowment, and sponsored research also increased, but not at the same rate. The upshot was an ever-deepening financial crisis.

The most basic cause of this difficult situation was probably the financial overoptimism which permeated most American universities, including Johns Hopkins, in the flush times of the mid-1960's. Although there were wiser heads who foresaw the coming debacle, a general mood of sanguinity was prevalent at all levels of the faculty and administration, and it took a long time for the danger signals to be correctly perceived. Retrenchment efforts were begun late in 1970, but by that time the University was headed for the greatest deficit in its history, a situation necessitating the spending of carefully husbanded reserves. There was much doubt, division, and uncertainty prevalent early in 1971, and much of this eventually landed at the president's door. Dr. Gordon submitted his resignation to the board of trustees on March 12. The executive committee of the board accepted the resignation, effective on the appointment of a successor, but in any event by June 30, 1972. In a statement to the press board chairman Robert D. H. Harvey said: "The action of the executive committee was taken with great regret. Dr. Gordon's leadership spanned a period of grave crisis for American institutions of higher learning. Many problems remain for solution, but Dr. Gordon has made substantial prog-

* There was much justification for a large increase in administrative personnel, since the relationship with the federal government required a much higher level of administrative support, and a large fund-raising campaign associated with the approaching University centennial was getting under way.

ress in charting a course for the University's future and in overcoming its serious financial problems. The committee feels deep appreciation and gratitude for Dr. Gordon's service."

No sooner had the March 12 announcement of Dr. Gordon's resignation been made than all segments of the University community began to concentrate on the question of the succession. It was generally realized that the selection of a permanent president would be a long and time-consuming task. Meanwhile, among students, faculty, administrators, and board members, a consensus developed that the best possible course for Johns Hopkins in a time of crisis would be to persuade former President Milton S. Eisenhower to come out of retirement and accept the role of leadership on an interim basis. At the age of seventy-one the veteran administrator was extremely reluctant to take on this arduous and relatively thankless task, but his sense of duty and dedication to the University were strong, and he agreed to return for a limited period. His appointment was announced at a press conference on March 25 and took effect April 5.*

Ten days after his reassumption of the burdens of office, Dr. Eisenhower addressed a special convocation of faculty, students, and staff, which filled the Shriver Hall auditorium to overflowing. Enthusiasm ran high in an audience which well realized how much energy, intelligence, and zeal this man had dedicated to the welfare of Johns Hopkins. Dr. Eisenhower in no way minimized the problems of the institution which he termed "so serious, so ominous, that they can be solved only with the complete cooperation of all who make up the Hopkins community." He pointed out that the cash deficit for fiscal 1971 would be more than $4.5 million, and proceeded to outline a number of retrenchment measures designed to bring a runaway financial situation under control. As he well knew, budget cuts involving a variety of administrative offices, academic departments, and auxiliary enterprises would be painful,

* Campus wags referred to Dr. Eisenhower's reassumption of the presidency as the Second Coming.

unpopular and vitally necessary. Looking ahead, the president proposed a substantial increase in the size of the undergraduate program, pointing out that, since his retirement in 1967, the student-faculty ratio had dropped from approximately thirteen to one to ten to one.* Citing the need for youth and female representation on the board of trustees, Dr. Eisenhower announced several changes in board by-laws and policies designed to accomplish this objective. He also promised no tuition increase during his interim term, and stressed his strong interest in providing the Homewood Campus with an adequate student union. Toward the end of his address Dr. Eisenhower said: "My energy is not what it was when I left here. But now that I have returned, my reluctance is forgotten and I shall personally do all I can to forward the interests of this distinguished institution for the short time I am here." The audience responded with a standing ovation.

△ △ △

In the ten months of his second presidency, Dr. Eisenhower demonstrated that his energy had suffered no noticeable diminution. In this time, as the *Johns Hopkins Magazine* put it, ". . . the University community realized that in his efforts to get the University moving again the veteran administrator had produced nothing short of a miracle." In the financial sphere there were the following accomplishments: the board of trustees pledged $1.2 million as a tribute to Milton Eisenhower's leadership; twelve corporations and foundations gave nearly $4 million to support a variety of programs; the State of Maryland, following an initiative originally developed by President Lincoln Gordon, granted $800,000 to the School of Medicine and $355,000 to Arts and Sciences; alumni contributed to a record Roll Call of $1,251,400; the Bologna Center of SAIS was strengthened by grants of $80,000 per year for five years; an endowed chair in the history of art was established through a $750,000 gift from the William R. Kenan, Jr. Charitable Trust.

Dr. Eisenhower's second presidency witnessed other important developments. At Homewood a blue ribbon committee

* It is noteworthy, however, that from the fall of 1970 to the fall of 1973, undergraduate enrollment increased by only 75 students—from 1,998 to 2,073.

began to review the undergraduate curriculum with the purpose of recommending desirable revisions. Another committee consisting of faculty members from Arts and Sciences and from Medicine began to consider a new program which could lead to the granting of the M.D. degree in a total of six years of undergraduate and graduate education. The president's cherished aim of providing the Homewood Campus with a functional student union moved toward realization as plans and specifications for the extensive renovation of Levering Hall and the construction of a large two-story wing to this building were drawn up.

△ △ △

At the Medical Institutions there were also significant events. Dr. Russell H. Morgan succeeded Dr. David E. Rogers as dean of the School of Medicine in November, 1971. Dr. Rogers, who had become dean upon the retirement of Dr. Thomas B. Turner in 1968, presided over the school at a time when "outreach" moved into high gear. A prepaid health-care plan was established by Johns Hopkins in the new city of Columbia, Maryland, and this was soon followed by a similar program in east Baltimore. As Dr. Rogers put it in an interview with the *Johns Hopkins Magazine*, this was not just preventive medicine but "genuine comprehensive medical care" in which "it's to our advantage to see you early, to prevent the very expensive features of illness, which in the main create the large bills because of high hospital-bed costs." In another important area, the trustees in September, 1971, approved, pending adequate funding, the creation of a new school of allied health sciences including nursing, medical and radiological technology, mental health counseling, and other paramedical disciplines.

From the beginning of Dr. Eisenhower's second presidency, a seven-member trustees' search and selection committee assisted by a seventeen-member advisory group made up of faculty, students, and alumni was hard at work screening scores of possible candidates for the University presidency. It was becoming apparent early in 1972 that the succession was imminent. In mid-January Dr. Eisenhower issued a farewell statement to the Johns Hopkins community summarizing the developments of the previous ten months, pointing out that on the crucial financial front progress could be measured by the fact that the deficit for fiscal 1972 would be less than the $2.4 million which had been budgeted and that the budgeted deficit for fiscal 1973 was down to $1.1 million.*

In his final words Dr. Eisenhower summed up his feelings on his second presidency:

> Candidly, I was quite content when I left here on June 30, 1967. It is no secret that I did not wish to return. When my conscience overcame my common sense and I acceded to the urgings of trustees and faculty members to serve again on an interim basis, I experienced what I was sure would be inevitable. I had to do mean things nearly every day, things that made me feel wretched. But with equal candor I say that if I now moved back to March 25, 1971, I would do again precisely what I have done. I would accept, I would have heartwarming cooperation, and I would leave about ten months later with a feeling of genuine friendship for all of you.

In addition to the great library which bears his name, Dr. Eisenhower's memorials at the University include: annual student-managed symposia on various problems of foreign and domestic policy, which, since their inception in 1968, have involved a host of distinguished participants from many walks of life; and the Milton S. Eisenhower gold medal, which the trustees grant on rare occasions to an individual who has contributed outstandingly to the welfare of the University.

O n January 20, 1972, the trustees elected Steven Muller the tenth president of Johns Hopkins. Dr. Muller, who assumed the burdens of office on February 1, had come to Johns Hopkins as provost at the beginning of Dr. Eisenhower's interim presidency. He quickly impressed faculty, administrators, and students alike with his keen grasp of the

* The actual deficit for fiscal 1972 was less than $1.8 million and that for 1973 was only $700,000.

University's problems and his energetic and no-nonsense approach to their solutions.

Dr. Muller graduated from U.C.L.A. in 1948 and was a Rhodes Scholar from 1949 to 1951. He received his Ph.D. degree in political science from Cornell University in 1958 and was director of that institution's Center for International Studies from 1961 until 1966. From 1966 to 1971 he was Cornell's vice-president for public affairs. At forty-four, he became the youngest president of Johns Hopkins since Daniel Coit Gilman. In a statement following the election, board chairman Robert D. H. Harvey pointed out that "a long and intensive search process" had convinced the trustees that Dr. Muller possessed "great vitality and imagination, a keen intellect and a proven ability to administer a complex university."

In his inaugural address in Shriver Hall, February 22, 1972, Dr. Muller touched on several significant themes, asserting: "Our heritage at Hopkins is that we are small and superb. We must continue to earn that reputation." Pointing out that the necessary course for the University "lies along the fine line between public regulation and public control, between public assistance and public ownership," he stated his conviction of the advantages of privacy: "We have at least the freedom to choose among alternatives, restricted as that choice may be, rather than to have our decisions dictated to us by public bodies."

In setting an agenda for the future, President Muller stressed the importance of finding "a more satisfying and compelling definition for the mission of undergraduate teaching . . .", of preserving "a sound foundation for research and advanced scholarship . . .", of finding ways "to increase our means and learn to live effectively within them . . .", of promoting self-government "so that no voice is stifled nor any interest ignored . . .", and of gaining "the affection as well as the respect of our neighbors in our own community."

Toward the end of his address the new president emphasized the historic mission of the true university:

> Universities . . . are . . . profoundly human in the natural or animal sense. Into them pour the young, full of passion and natural appetites. The same passions and appetites course through the rest of us. No man is pure reason. A university

therefore is a deeply human organism in which reason and nature strive together as in mankind itself. Sometimes the flesh is martyred by reason, sometimes reason is martyred by human passion. Passion in the service of reason can lead to the utmost in human achievement. Reason in the service of passion can lead to the torment of men and women by each other. At universities, reason has a special priority.

In closing Dr. Muller made a plea for humor and toleration:

Finally, let us rejoice in our humanity and in the special opportunities that the University offers. Humor and laughter are also uniquely human. A human community without them is cursed. As we conclude this rare occasion that brings us together, let us resolve to strive, not only for achievement, but for the grace of laughter and kindness. We are here and now and able—and insecure and fragile—and alive—let us together make the utmost of what we are and what we have.

As the final pages of this narrative are composed in mid-summer, 1974, it appears clear that the momentum reestablished in University affairs in the second Eisenhower presidency has continued and even accelerated since the inauguration of Steven Muller. As the centennial year of 1976 approaches, Johns Hopkins presents the picture of an incredibly complex social institution totally committed to its original missions of teaching and research but in a world which bears little resemblance to that of Daniel Coit Gilman and his founding faculty.

Since taking office, much of Dr. Muller's time and the time of key administrators has been devoted to dealing with ever-present financial problems. This will occasion no surprise to those familiar with the private university's peculiar vulnerability to the problems of inflation, fluctuating enrollment patterns, and uncertain federal support. Dr. Muller and his staff have attacked the financial problem with determination and imagination. The success that has been achieved has been extremely impressive.

As noted earlier, the deficit for fiscal 1973 was a rather

In April and May of 1969, President Gordon was confronted with student demands and protests, including a sit-in at Homewood House.

Dr. Eisenhower addressed a special convocation ten days after returning to the presidency in 1971, warning of the serious financial problems facing the University and outlining what remedies were needed.

The School of Advanced International Studies became a graduate division of the University in 1950. Since then, the School and its Center in Bologna, Italy, have trained several thousand specialists in international relations to serve the government and private business organizations.

The 106-foot, aluminum-hulled catamaran Ridgely Warfield *provides a stable platform for important oceanographic research carried on by the University's Chesapeake Bay Institute.*

In 1974, the Johns Hopkins lacrosse team defeated the University of Maryland to win the N.C.A.A. national title for the first time since the championships began in 1971.

The Applied Physics Laboratory continues to concentrate on national defense, as well as delving into research in outer space. APL scientists have developed navigational satellites, such as the one shown, for the Navy's world-wide, all-weather navigational system.

In June of 1974, ground was broken and demolition began for the Hospital's $47.5 million rebuilding program, including a patient care and teaching facility, the Comprehensive Cancer Center, and improved facilities for diagnostic radiology and materials management.

The Hopkins Union, completed in 1974, features a transparent-domed rathskeller, theatre, darkrooms, and music practice rooms.

Inaugurated as president in February 1972, Dr. Steven Muller quickly moved to launch the $100 million Hopkins Hundreds campaign and to mobilize the resources to assure the University's well-being during its Centennial era.

modest $700,000, considerably less than had been anticipated. For fiscal 1974, the trustees gratefully approved a balanced budget with expenditures (exclusive of APL) expected to total about $104.8 million. As of this writing, it appears that this budget will turn out to have been balanced for the first time since 1967–68. A balanced budget of $120.3 million has also been projected for 1974–75. This $15.5 million increase in one year represents both the growing scale of University operations and the inexorable toll of inflation.

Important to the increasing financial health of Johns Hopkins has been a gratifying level of alumni support. The Annual Roll Call topped $2 million for the first time in 1972–73, and this achievement was repeated in 1973–74. Also significant has been the aid provided by the state of Maryland, which totaled $940,000 in 1973–74, and is expected to rise under a new allocation formula to about $1.6 million in 1975–76.

On Commemoration Day, February 22, 1973, President Muller launched the largest and most significant fund-raising campaign in the history of the Johns Hopkins institutions. A joint endeavor of the University and the Hospital, the campaign is called "Hopkins Hundreds," to symbolize two of the drive's major objectives: to bring to one hundred the number of permanently endowed chairs in the University, and to make possible a $100 million rebuilding of facilities at The Johns Hopkins Hospital. Specifically, the goals to be attained include the raising of $20 million in private funds for the Hospital, with the remaining $80 million to be borrowed and repaid out of income for patient care; and $50 million to provide 50 new named professorships at $1 million each, thereby bringing the total number of endowed chairs at the University to one hundred. Other objectives of the campaign include $6 million in program support for the new School of Health Services, $4 million to support the educational programs of the School of Medicine and the School of Hygiene and Public Health, $15 million for additional endowment and new teaching and research facilities at Homewood, and $3 million for library expansion, renovation of existing facilities, and student support endowment at the School of Advanced International Studies. In announcing the campaign, President Muller made his determination clear: "It is time for major private institutions in this country to say aloud that they intend to survive, that they will survive, and by so doing to set an example for all privately funded institutions be they schools, churches, hospitals, symphonies, or universities."

One year later, at the Hopkins Hundreds dinner on the eve of Commemoration Day, 1974, Dr. Muller announced that the intensive fund-raising efforts of the University and Hospital had thus far been crowned with tremendous success. The halfway mark had been reached. Slightly more than $50 million had been received, one of the most successful one-year campaigns in the history of American philanthropy. More than $10 million of this amount was committed by the trustees of the University and Hospital. The total included twelve endowed chairs for the University and two pledges of more than a million dollars each for the Hospital.*

Throughout history the most significant fact about great institutions has been their ability to evolve and adapt in the face of changing circumstances, while preserving the essential spirit or soul which made them great in the first place. As Johns Hopkins enters upon its centennial era, it cannot be found wanting in either of these criteria. Although change and adaptation are ever-present realities, the soul of this great institution is intact. This truth can be observed in all the divisions of the University with their extraordinary diversity and complexity.

Since the winter of 1972, life and work at Homewood have exhibited signs of great vitality. Student life provides an excellent example. The student-managed annual Milton S. Eisenhower Symposium, inaugurated in 1967, has attracted growing attention and respect. The Symposium of 1972 revolved around the basic theme, "Creativity: The Moving Force of Society," and attracted the talents of such participants as critic Clive Barnes, psychologist Jean Piaget, sociologist Nathan Glazer, composer Aaron Copeland, and novelist C. P. Snow. In 1973,

* In the summer of 1974 the number of new endowed chairs stood at fourteen.

the Symposium dealt with the well-chosen topic, "Living with Change," defined by student co-chairman David Yaffe as "the process by which the future invades our lives." Ranging over a wide spectrum of human experiences were the remarks of such luminaries as keynote speaker R. Buckminster Fuller, psychologist Alberta Siegel, historian Frank Manuel, environmentalist Barry Commoner, theologian Harvey Cox, deputy director-general of the World Health Organization T. A. Lambo, economist Kenneth Boulding, Senator Charles Percy, and author Isaac Asimov.

Another recent and imaginative endeavor of Hopkins undergraduates has been the production in 1972, 1973, and 1974 of the "3400 On Stage" contemporary festivals at Homewood. In this case "3400" refers not to the number of performers but to the address of the Homewood Campus at 3400 North Charles Street. Featuring varied events, activities, and exhibits spanning the arts and crafts, music, drama, sports, and academics, these April festivals have provided considerable "outreach" in that their main purpose has been to increase communication between the University and the surrounding community. Thousands of persons of all ages have enjoyed these events, and "3400 On Stage" seems well on the way to becoming a permanent item on the Homewood calendar.

Another recent festival at Homewood was "Next Step: A Festival of Women" held in February, 1974, and planned to precede the graduation in the spring of the first four-year co-educational class. Featuring addresses by poet Anne Sexton, actress Jane Fonda, black feminist Nan Bailey, civil rights advocate Yolanda Ford, and defeated gubernatorial candidate Sissy Farenthold, the purpose of the festival, according to co-chairperson Mindy Farber, was "to celebrate the presence of women on campus and demonstrate what their potential talents will contribute to the world at large."

Women students have become an increasingly important part of the Homewood scene since the fall of 1970. In 1973–74 there were 472 female undergraduate and 246 graduate students enrolled at Homewood, constituting 23 percent and 26 percent of these categories, respectively. According to a status report on women in the Arts and Sciences division issued in December, 1973, women held five places on the Student Council, the presidency of the Debate Council, the presidency of a service fraternity, and representation on several policy-making and problem-solving committees. Women are now eligible for R.O.T.C. scholarships and commission into the Army as second lieutenants. In 1973–74 seven freshman and sophomore women were enrolled in the Military Science I program.

In the spring of 1973 a series of meetings was held between representatives of Johns Hopkins and Goucher College to explore the possibilities of increased cooperation or outright merger of the two institutions. The problems involved in merger were so considerable that the trustees of Goucher finally decided against such a course, but they did decide to seek increased cooperation. What forms this may take remain to be seen, but possibilities include faculty exchanges, a cooperative B.A.–M.A. program, the creation of a women's center or institute, and expanded evening and summer programs.

△ △ △

The administration of Dr. Muller has emphasized an improvement in the quality of student life at Homewood. Following a recommendation of the blue ribbon Committee on Undergraduate Education mentioned above, the president appointed a dean of students for the division of Arts and Sciences in the spring of 1972. The dean of students now has responsibility for most areas of non-academic affairs such as student counseling, housing, health services and the psychological clinic, student activities, and the physical education program. Several important appointments have been made in this office, including a director of housing, a director of student affairs, and a director of the new student union.

In the summer of 1974, the new student union was completed, thereby fulfilling the desire Dr. Eisenhower so strongly expressed in 1971. This handsome building in modern style, containing large and small meeting rooms, offices for various student organizations, a small and intimate theatre, and a rathskeller where beer will be served, should bring about a decisive change for the better in the quality of student life at Homewood. Also relevant in this connection is the fact that Levering Hall has been completely renovated, including the

Great Hall, the cafeteria, and the lobby, which now contains a central information center capable of servicing the entire Homewood community.

For whatever one may make of it, the concern for improving the quality of student life is not one that would have particularly bothered Gildersleeve, Sylvester, Rowland, or Remsen. A great institution must adapt but not at the cost of its soul. The soul of Johns Hopkins has always involved the nurturing of the life of the mind in its most sublime manifestations. A brief treatment of some examples of this continuing mission at Homewood in the short span of time since Dr. Muller assumed the presidency may be illustrative.

In the spring of 1972, it was announced that during the summer an ancient cemetery near the Great Pyramid at Giza would be excavated by a team led by Hans Goedicke, noted Egyptologist, and head of the University's Department of Near Eastern Studies. Dr. Goedicke hoped that the work would yield new information about ancient Egyptian life and the problems of building the pyramids themselves. At about the same time, three members of the Homewood faculty: James S. Coleman, professor of social relations; Hans P. Eugster, professor of geology; and Saul Roseman, professor and chairman of the Department of Biology, were elected to membership in the prestigious National Academy of Sciences, bringing to fifteen the number of Johns Hopkins faculty members of this organization. A two-volume biography of the English artist Hogarth, the result of eleven years of research and study by English Department chairman Ronald Paulson, received national acclaim and a nomination for the National Book Award in the biography category.

In the fall of 1972, the *Johns Hopkins Journal* reported that "a major milepost in a long tradition of astrophysical research at Johns Hopkins will be reached in December when the Apollo 17 spacecraft is scheduled to go into orbit about the moon." This referred to the "most sensitive spectrometer ever flown in space," an instrument which was a joint endeavor of the

Homewood Physics Department and the Applied Physics Laboratory. The *Journal* also announced that the Department of Geography and Environmental Engineering had received a $1.2 million contract from the Edison Electric Institute to continue a long-term study on the problem of thermal pollution, with particular emphasis on the effects of power plant discharges on living organisms in the water. This research continues a long tradition in water resources investigation at Homewood, personified by men like Abel Wolman and John C. Geyer. The Department of Psychology reported progress on programs sponsored by the Spencer Foundation of Chicago aimed at discovering junior high school students in the Baltimore area with high aptitude in quantitative areas of math and science, as well as in verbal and humanistic skills, in order to accelerate the progress of their education.

In the spring of 1973, the University released the news that John Barth, distinguished novelist and alumnus of the old Department of Writing, Speech, and Drama, would return to Johns Hopkins with a joint appointment as professor in the Writing Seminars and the Department of English. The latter department would also be joined by Hugh Kenner, a leading critic and author of works on T. S. Eliot, James Joyce, Samuel Beckett, and Ezra Pound. Scientists from the Chesapeake Bay Institute affiliated with the Department of Earth and Planetary Sciences announced the discovery in the Bay of a great river valley, now filled with mud and sand, which once carried the waters of the Susquehanna River as it sought an outlet in the sea. Also reported in the spring was a grant of $100,000 from the Westinghouse Educational Foundation in support of major innovations in the undergraduate program in electrical engineering.

The *Johns Hopkins Journal* in the summer of 1973 carried the news of a number of important developments in the Department of Chemistry. An overall plan of modernization was in the process of being carried out. Central to this was a complete renovation of Remsen Hall, badly needed in a building which was built a half-century earlier. Two major laboratories had already been recreated, and one of these, the John M. Olin Organic Chemistry Laboratory, was described by department faculty as the finest facility of its kind anywhere. Also involved were significant changes in the curriculum with separate freshman chemistry courses tailored for three kinds of students: physical science majors; well-prepared premedical students, and less well-prepared premedical students.

Also in the summer of 1973, it was made known that a young Hopkins paleobiologist, Steven Stanley, had propounded a persuasive explanation (unfortunately too complex to be considered here) for the explosive speed on a geologic time scale of the creation of higher life forms during the Cambrian Period. Two more members of the Homewood faculty were elected to the National Academy of Sciences, and Maurice Mandelbaum, Andrew Mellon Professor of Philosophy and one of Homewood's greatest teacher-scholars, was elected a Fellow of the American Academy of Arts and Sciences, the second oldest learned society in the country.

It was reported in the winter of 1974 that an imaginative and effective way of teaching freshman physics by permitting students to advance at their own pace, through the use of tutors, had been developed by a thirty-four-year-old associate professor in the department. A project designed to seek to define the factors that go into social standing or prestige of American families was announced as being funded by the National Institute of Mental Health and directed by Peter H. Rossi, professor of social relations and research director of the Center for Metropolitan Planning and Research. James F. Bell, professor of solid mechanics, became the first person to write, without collaborators, an entire volume in the *Handbuch der Physik* series, a primary reference source used by scientists all over the world. The *Journal* made known the experiments of Alphonse Chapanis, professor of psychology, in the important but little understood area of man-computer relations. "The one thing that's come out of these experiments so far that's really surprising to us," said Dr. Chapanis, "is the power of the voice channel. All of what we call the hard-copy modes—anything involving a piece of paper—are typically very much slower than any mode that involves voice."

The "new" history was featured in a *Journal* article in the spring of 1974. Professor Robert Forster of the history department termed the new approach "history from below," arguing that "what is new is that we're beginning to get at the masses of people who didn't leave behind any direct written evidence. . . . This gets into the area of social psychology where you try to deal with the little guy and discover his attitudes, customs and motives . . ." Such interests on the part of a number of the history faculty have resulted in the establishment of the Atlantic History and Culture program, whose purpose is the comparative study of social institutions in the four continents bordering the Atlantic Ocean. Because of the importance of anthropology to this program, the department in 1973 approached the program's original sponsor, the Rockefeller Foundation, with a proposal to establish a new Department of Anthropology at Johns Hopkins. The result has been a four-year $490,000 grant for that purpose and the hiring of a highly regarded young anthropologist as chairman.

Among honors accruing to Homewood faculty members in 1973–74 were the following: Clifford Truesdell, professor of rational mechanics, was appointed to the Lincean Professorship, one of Italy's highest academic honors. Stanley Corrsin, professor of fluid mechanics, received an honorary degree from the University of Lyon. Francis J. Pettijohn, professor emeritus of earth and planetary sciences, was awarded the 1974 Twenhofel Medal by the Society of Economic Paleontologists and Mineralogists. William Fastie, adjunct research professor of physics, received the Exceptional Scientific Achievement Medal of the National Aeronautics and Space Administration for this contributions to the United States space exploration program. Alphonse Chapanis, professor of psychology, received the 1973 Paul M. Fitts Award of the Human Factors Society for contributions to the education and training of human factors specialists.

The events chronicled here represent only a very small percentage of the total teaching and research activities of the Homewood faculty for a period of a little more than two years. Nonetheless, such a potpourri may hopefully provide some indication of the range, depth, and distinction of the efforts of some of the most eminent scholars and scientists in this or any other country.

Actually an independent operation, the Johns Hopkins University Press has been intimately associated with the research activities of the Arts and Sciences faculty since Daniel Coit Gilman presided at its birth in 1878. As the oldest continuously operating university press in the country, it has long been known for the quality of its publications. In the past quarter century, however, the Press has undergone a degree of growth which today makes it fairly big business by almost any definition. This growth has coincided with the directorship of Harold E. Ingle, who retired in July, 1974, after 26 years of dedicated leadership. When Mr. Ingle came to the Press in 1948, the annual production consisted of about a dozen books representing a sales volume of $75,000. There was a staff of four with a "warehouse" set up in two World War II Quonset huts located in the light shafts of Gilman Hall. Today the Press has a staff of 50, operates its own off-campus warehouse, and in 1974 published 75 new books with sales of nearly $1.9 million. Foreign sales now account for about 20 percent of the total. There is a Press branch office in London and sales representatives all over the world. During Mr. Ingle's tenure as director, many highly significant works have been published. Some have even become best sellers. One project, which may be mentioned because of its intrinsic interest, is the planned twenty-volume set of the edited papers of Dwight D. Eisenhower, five of which have been issued as of this writing.

Although the concentration in the final section of this brief history has been upon developments at Homewood, attention must also be given to other divisions of the University. In the Evening College several significant changes in curriculum and structure have been made. For the first time the College has been authorized by its Advisory Board to grant the Master of Science degree with specialized areas of concentration in education. This has made possible a greater responsiveness to the needs of educational specialists in reading, counseling and guidance, and adult education. Approval has also been granted to offer graduate programs in business and the administrative sciences. A Division of Special Programs has been created to handle multidisciplinary and interdivisional degree programs, such as, for example, the M.S. in Urban Planning. The Advisory Board, which governs the Evening College, has been reconstituted to make it more specifically representative of its own academic-administrative and instructional faculty, and a core of full-time faculty members holding appointments within the College has been authorized. An off-campus Center has been established at Columbia, Maryland, in addition to the one already functioning at the Applied Physics Laboratory.

△ △ △

In September, 1972, one of the most significant developments in the history of the Johns Hopkins Medical Institutions was made known to the press. Effective October 1, Steven Muller, president of the University, would also become president of The Johns Hopkins Hospital, thus binding the University and the Hospital together under a single leadership for the first time since Daniel Coit Gilman acted briefly as chief executive of the Hospital in 1889. William E. McGuirk, Jr., chairman of the Hospital Board of Trustees, commented cogently that the two institutions had been intimately associated since their founding, and that "the rapid and extensive development of joint School of Medicine and Hospital programs in recent years makes it highly appropriate that the presidencies of the institutions now be combined." He added that the trustees believed that "combining the presidencies under Dr. Muller will make the Hospital even stronger and that it will simplify the administrative coordination of the Johns Hopkins medical institutions, enabling swift response to developing needs." Recognizing the virtual impossibility of administering both institutions on a day-to-day basis, Dr. Muller announced the appointment of Dr. Robert Heyssel, professor of medicine and former director of the Office of Health Care Programs, as executive vice-president and director of the Hospital. The growing cohesion between the two institutions symbolized by this development is made quite explicit in the Hopkins Hundreds campaign, a joint effort of the University and the Hospital.

△ △ △

The newest division of the University, the School of Health Services, authorized by the trustees in 1971, opened in the fall of 1973 with a class of 35 students. The fledgling school received a powerful boost early in that year through a $3 million grant from the Robert Wood Johnson Foundation. The initial curriculum, the Health Associate Program, is designed to provide the third and fourth years of a baccalaureate degree program and emphasizes human biology, social sciences, the humanities, and clinical skills to prepare the health associates to be practitioners capable of dealing with the common health problems of children, adults, and families. Plans for the immediate future are directed toward the creation of a nursing education program, and longer range projections include programs in environmental and industrial health as well as in health services management. There seems little doubt but that demands for a more rational allocation of our scarce health care resources, involving the extensive use of health practitioners and technicians in a number of areas, will continue to grow, and that the School of Health Services, under the innovative leadership of Dean Malcolm Peterson, will make a vital contribution.

△ △ △

In the fall of 1973, construction plans for the first phase of a massive Hospital redevelopment program were approved. While the program involves the Hospital most directly, it is closely related to the teaching and research activities of all the Johns Hopkins Medical Institutions. Groundbreaking ceremonies were held in June, 1974, and featured remarks by Dr. Muller, Senator Charles McC. Mathias, and Dr. Robert M. Heyssel. Both the federal and state governments were instrumental in providing funding for the $12.5 million Johns Hopkins Comprehensive Cancer Center, which is the keystone of the total redevelopment project. This oncology center has been designated by the National Cancer Institute as a regional research and treatment center, combining both research laboratories and patient care facilities. The total redevelopment program of the Hospital will take place in a series of building stages over the next 20 to 30 years. This initial segment is scheduled for completion in 1976.

There is no intention or possibility at this point of dealing with the vast range of research activities at the Medical Institutions in the past three years. A very few, however, of great significance will be singled out. In March, 1973, *Science* magazine reported that Dr. Solomon H. Snyder, professor of pharmacology and of psychiatry at the School of Medicine, and graduate student Ms. Candace B. Pert had identified the site where heroin and other opiates act in the brain. This research may have important practical implications for the treatment of heroin addicts and may also enable scientists to find out the normal function for these opiate receptors and thereby uncover the fundamental mechanism whereby narcotics produce their effects in man.

Also in March, 1973, it was announced that Dr. MacKenzie Walser, professor of pharmacology and experimental therapeutics, had developed a new drug treatment for chronic kidney failure which can replace or delay the need for renal dialysis. This treatment, which is of enormous importance to many kidney patients, employs synthetic drugs combined with a low-protein diet to provide necessary nourishment without producing the waste products their kidneys cannot remove. In the studies described by Dr. Walser in the *Journal of Clinical Investigation*, six out of ten patients with severe kidney failure showed improvement and were able to go without renal dialysis. A project to screen 10,000 men for early detection of lung cancer, supported by a $629,652 research contract from the National Cancer Institute, was featured in the press in October, 1973. The twelve- to fifteen-year study by the Medical Institutions is designed to evaluate the effects of new detection, diagnosis, location, and treatment methods of lung tumors on the survival of lung cancer patients. Pilot studies conducted by Johns Hopkins researchers indicate that these new techniques can identify small lung tumors before they show up on conventional chest x-rays.

An example of the fruitful cooperation which has developed between the Johns Hopkins Medical Institutions and the Applied Physics Laboratory has been the revolutionary rechargeable heart pacemaker. The result of five years of cooperative research between Robert Fischell, a physicist at APL, and Kenneth B. Lewis, assistant professor of medicine, the stainless steel pacemaker, about the size of a flat cigarette lighter, recharges painlessly through the skin via a special battery. As of May, 1974, more than 300 of these heart pacers had been implanted in patients in the United States and abroad. The pacemaker's life span is at least 20 years and probably limitless. The development is an indication of ways funds spent to develop equipment for space technology can benefit medicine. The long-lasting, rechargeable battery grew out of APL's experience in building batteries for spacecraft.

A significant administrative change was made in the structure of the Medical Institutions early in 1973. Effective March 1, Dr. Russell H. Morgan, dean of the School of Medicine since 1971, became vice-president for health divisions. Dr. Morgan's new responsibilities involve the coordination of the administrative activities of the University's three health-related divisions: the School of Medicine, the School of Hygiene and Public Health, and the School of Health Services. In the summer of 1974, Dr. Morgan continues to act as dean of the School of Medicine, while a search committee appointed by President Muller is actively engaged in seeking a successor.

In the School of Hygiene and Public Health, the untiring and skillful efforts of Dean John C. Hume and his associates have overcome the precarious financial situation which existed in 1972 and brought about a balanced budget together with increased enrollment. A new Department of Environmental Health Sciences was established early in 1974, consolidating teaching and research which had long been carried out in other departments in five major areas: environmental and occupational medicine; radiation health; environmental toxicology; environmental physiology, and environmental engineering. Two new divisions have been created in the Department of Public Health Administration, the division of health education and the division of operations research and health systems analysis.

Some of the most significant research carried out in the School in the past three years has been by researchers in the Department of Population Dynamics. Dr. Melvin Zelnik and Dr. John Kantner have conducted a highly influential survey of the sexual habits of American teenagers. Their conclusions generally indicate the need for more adequate and far-reaching programs of sex education. The Department has also been intimately involved in helping such nations as Bangladesh, Taiwan, Turkey, and Pakistan develop and implement family planning programs.

Funded by a grant from HEW, Professor Charles D. Flagle of the Department of Public Health Administration is currently carrying out a highly important study of health care delivery systems for the elderly. Also in progress in the summer of 1974 is a study by Dr. Wallace Mandell of the Department of Mental Hygiene in the area of narcotics addiction. Dr. Mandell is studying 1,500 addicts in an effort to find factors which will increase the likelihood of successful treatment. The same department has also initiated a demonstration training program for alcoholism counselors. Researchers in the Department of Epidemiology have continued examination of the effects of oral contraceptives and have concluded that women using "the pill" incur a nine times greater risk of stroke than non-users.

At the Applied Physics Laboratory, that remote, little understood, but highly productive division of the University in Howard County, several significant developments in technology in the past three years can be reported.

The Laboratory's background and long experience in applying modern signal and data processing techniques to the radar detection and tracking of aircraft, missiles, and other air threats to the Fleet have proved applicable in substantial measure to the Coast Guard's need for more effective surveillance and control of harbor areas and to improved FAA terminal air traffic control. Working closely with Coast Guard management and operators at the San Francisco Deep Craft Waterway System, APL engineers have designed and installed a vessel traffic system that assures safe separation of vessels of all sizes through automated all-weather surveillance, traffic analysis and display, and communications services. This radar and radio system is applicable to other ports and harbors, and the same essential technology is being applied under a contract with the Federal Aviation Administration for the surveillance of aircraft and the prevention of collision at major air terminals.

In recent years there has been increasing utilization of the APL-developed Transit Navigation Satellite System, which allows users to determine their latitude and longitude to an accuracy of better than 0.1 nautical mile. Shipboard navigation equipment developed at the Laboratory is used by many Navy vessels, oceanographic ships, and in special applications such as the recovery of astronauts and world-wide charting of the earth's magnetic field by specially equipped aircraft. Other applications of this system have included a Miniceiver, developed for installation in free-floating buoys used in obtaining weather and ocean data, and TRANSIM, a new low-cost navigation set designed to meet the needs of commercial shipping and pleasure craft. The fruitful partnership between the Laboratory and the Medical Institutions in the development of the rechargeable heart pacemaker has already been noted.

A t the School of Advanced International Studies, Dr. Robert E. Osgood succeeded Dr. Francis O. Wilcox as dean in May, 1973. Dr. Osgood joined the SAIS faculty in 1961 and prior to his appointment as dean was director of the Washington Center of Foreign Policy Research. He continues to hold the Christian A. Herter professorship of American foreign policy. At the Bologna Center, there was also a key administrative change when Dr. Simon Serfaty, a SAIS graduate and former member of the Department of Political Science at U.C.L.A., was appointed director in June, 1972, upon the retirement of Professor C. Grove Haines.

Since the inception of the Hopkins Hundreds campaign, the School has been the recipient of three endowed chairs, bringing the total of named professorships to seven. The new chairs are the Arthur Vining Davis Foundation and the William H. Donner Foundation Chair in Canadian Studies, the Edward B. Burling Chair in International Law and Organization, and the Jacob Blaustein Chair in International Organizations.

The Ocean Policy Project at SAIS was established in 1972 with a grant from the National Science Foundation. Conducted under the auspices of the Washington Center of Foreign Policy Research, the Project conducts a special multidisciplinary seminar as well as policy-relevant research. Currently research efforts are focused on the policy options available to the United States in the Third United Nations Conference on the Law of the Sea. The Project provides periodic briefings to government officials and members of Congress, as well as staff assistance to public interest groups, colleges and universities, and the press.

Another recent offshoot of the Washington Center of Foreign Policy Research has been the Institute of International Social Science Research, established in 1973 and supported by an endowment from the Rockefeller Brothers Fund and other private grants. In its research the Institute utilizes scientific opinion polling techniques at both the public and private levels, and it prepares papers, reports, and books on the psychological dynamics that influence political and social behavior in the United States and abroad. The Institute is a valuable resource to the Center through its scientific interpretation of poll data. The Center, in turn, provides analysis of the political context, international and domestic, within which such interpretation takes place.

In this necessarily sketchy consideration of the myriad of research and teaching activities in the various schools and divisions of the University, a final word should be said about the growing impact of the Center for Metropolitan Planning and Research, informally known as the Metro Center. Since its removal to the Homewood campus in July, 1972, the Center, under the dynamic leadership of Dr. Jack Fisher, has become a true catalyst for a rational, research-oriented approach to urban problems. The research and educational programs mentioned earlier have continued to be basic to the Center's operation. In 1974 there are about twenty major research projects under way, and these support some twenty-five graduate students from various departments. The internship programs for undergraduates are flourishing and are now operating with the participation of four other area colleges. The International Fellowship Program, which Dr. Fisher regards as "the really distinctive feature of our whole urban studies program," brings from twelve to fifteen junior and senior fellows to this country each year. As Fisher puts it, "The predominant thrust of the program is Europe, because the problems of the United States and Europe are very much alike."

Community service is a rapidly evolving area of the Metro Center's concern, and is potentially controversial as academic types become involved sometimes reluctantly and sometimes eagerly in making judgments on complex urban problems. Examples of growing "outreach" are two seminar series which have been recently organized. One of these is held monthly in cooperation with the Greater Baltimore Committee, a group of businessmen primarily responsible for the major renewal efforts that have taken place in downtown Baltimore. This seminar brings Metro Center staff together with twenty to twenty-five Baltimoreans who represent the corporate and business communities. The other seminar series was organized by the Center in cooperation with Baltimore City Council President Walter S. Orlinsky '60. It involves City Council members and state legislators from the metropolitan area and attempts to deal in some depth with such problems as the structure of metropolitan areas, transportation planning, legal and financial aspects of public education, and housing. The dialogue that has resulted from these exchanges has been stimulating and constructive, both to the businessmen and elected representatives on the one hand, and to the Metro Center staff on the other.

President Muller summarized the rationale for the University's increasing involvement in urban problems early in 1974 in a *Johns Hopkins Magazine* article on the Center:

> What seems to me self-evident is that we should not, and have decided that we will not, ignore the major area of metropolitan studies. Our principal reason for being in this area is obviously academic. This is a field which is inter-disciplinary, where a lot of our faculty have concerns, and the Metro Center makes sense, first and foremost, from the standpoint of an academic operation.
>
> Once you have that, though, then it seems to me that you've got to realize you have assets that are potentially relevant to your own community, and you've got to try to make a marriage between what the community needs and those assets. So far this has gone so well that for the first time, I guess, there is a really constructive dialogue between quite a large sampling of people in the area and people in the University. This is being treated as something new, because apparently this kind of dialogue hasn't taken place before. I find it in some ways ironic that people are responding so wholeheartedly to something that I think should have been the rule all along.

This statement of Dr. Muller is highly significant, for it provides an indication, at least to this writer, of an evolving theme for the University in the 1970's. It has been noted that a main theme of the Eisenhower years was the bringing of cohesion, coordination, and unity out of the incredible diversity of a tremendously complex institution. In the time since January, 1972, when Dr. Muller assumed the presidency, the search for unity and cohesion has not ceased. It is evident in many of the developments described in the preceding pages. To cite just a few examples, we may note the vesting of the presidencies of the University and the Hospital in a single individual, the ever-increasing cooperation between the Applied Physics Laboratory and other divisions of Johns Hopkins, and the multidisciplinary activities of the Center for Metropolitan Planning and

Research. Other examples would be easy to find, but it is not necessary to belabor the point. What seems clear is that the rationale for the search for unity out of diversity has subtly shifted. In the sixties it seemed imperative in order to avoid fragmentation and chaos in what had become a large multiversity. The tendencies toward "outreach" sometimes seemed to conflict with this goal. In the seventies it seems that hard-won cohesion is increasingly being used in the service of "outreach" —an idea whose time has obviously come.

△ △ △

The evidence abounds. Whether it be the involvement of the School of Medicine in the comprehensive medical care programs in east Baltimore and Columbia, the involvement of the School of Hygiene in family planning, the increasing participation of SAIS faculty and students in the practical aspects of foreign policy formulation, the growing tendency of APL research achievements to be applied to civilian problems, the seminars of the Metro Center, the "3400 On Stage" festivals at Homewood, or the concept of "history from below," it is apparent that a new spirit is abroad in the University. The ivory tower or elitist concept of the University, still strong in many quarters and probably vitally necessary to an institution with the traditions of Johns Hopkins, seems to have given much ground to the relatively new notion of a University actively involved in seeking real-life solutions to the problems which plague mankind. This seems to be the evolving theme of the seventies.

Nearly five years ago the University began making plans for its centennial observance. In late 1969 President Lincoln Gordon appointed Dr. Ferdinand Hamburger, Jr. to serve as director of centennial planning. Dr. Hamburger, long-time professor and chairman of the Department of Electrical Engineering, has been associated with Johns Hopkins as undergraduate, graduate student, and faculty member for more than fifty years. In 1971, he was largely responsible for the establishment of the University archives, which now occupies space in the Eisenhower Library and provides a treasure trove of material relating to the history of Johns Hopkins. Under Dr. Hamburger's steady and devoted direction, final plans are now taking shape for a variety of festivities, meetings, and impressive academic events which will celebrate the University's one hundredth birthday in 1976. All constituencies of Johns Hopkins will take part, including students, faculty, employees, trustees, administrators, and alumni, as well as many dignitaries from this country and abroad.

On December 24, 1973, at a simple ceremony in Green Mount Cemetery, President Muller, accompanied by Mayor William Donald Schaefer of Baltimore, Robert D. H. Harvey, chairman of the University trustees, other members of the University and Hospital administrations, and descendants of Johns Hopkins, placed a wreath at the grave of Mr. Johns Hopkins on the occasion of the one hundredth anniversary of his death. Speaking of the founder, Dr. Muller said: "As we salute a life that brought so much to life, we dedicate ourselves anew to the spirit of compassion and love of mankind that is the most enduring and endearing part of our founding. We thank and cherish the memory of Mr. Johns Hopkins."

Commencement ceremonies at Johns Hopkins have always been interesting and colorful in the literal sense because the academic regalia of the graduates and faculty represent so many different degrees, institutions, and branches of learning. The Commencement of May 24, 1974, was no exception. More than 2,100 students were awarded degrees in the ceremonies at Homewood. Of these, typically, nearly two-thirds were either master's degrees or doctorates from the Arts and Sciences divisions, the Evening College, the School of Medicine, the School of Hygiene and Public Health, and the School of Advanced International Studies. Honorary degrees were awarded to Benjamin M. Baker, professor emeritus of medicine at the School of Medicine and a pioneer in the under-standing, treatment, and prevention of coronary artery disease; to Frederic C. Lane, professor emeritus of history at Homewood and a leading scholar of the Italian Renaissance; to John M. Olin, honorary chairman of the board and a director of Olin Corporation, who has been a trustee of Johns Hopkins for over twenty years; and to Rafael Hernandez Colon, the youngest governor in Puerto Rico's history and an alumnus of the Hopkins class of '56.

Governor Hernandez Colon, in the Commencement address, discussed the world's state of "chronic economic vulnerability," runaway population growth, and world-wide food shortages, arguing that national priorities and personal life styles must be changed "in order to save our small planet from ourselves." As he said, "There is little time to waste." Despite these sobering thoughts, the weekend ended on a triumphant note as the Johns Hopkins lacrosse team defeated Washington and Lee the next day and thereby earned a shot at the NCAA champion-ship.

The following Saturday was Homecoming, and this writer made his annual pilgrimage to Homewood for the occasion. The campus was serene and beautiful on a magnificent spring day. The crab cake and beer feast in the White Athletic Center was delightful, and the trooping of the classes was impressive evidence of the loyalty of thousands of alumni. All eyes, how-ever, were soon focused on Homewood Field, where the annual lacrosse match between the Blue Jays and the Terrapins of the University of Maryland was about to take place. *Aficionados* agree that this was one of the greatest lacrosse games ever played. No doubt the fact that this was Coach Bob Scott's last season at the helm affected the outcome as the Blue Jays, play-ing with both skill and aggression, defeated the defending champion Terrapins by a score of 17–13. Three weeks later, Johns Hopkins repeated this performance in the NCAA playoff game at Rutgers, defeating Maryland 17–12 in a superb show of stick handling, and winning the national championship for the thirtieth time. It indeed seemed in this spring of 1974 that God was in his heaven and all was right with the Hopkins world.

As Johns Hopkins enters upon its centennial era, it is only natural that thoughts turn to the long and impressive history of this great institution. With a current budget of $120 million, most of which goes for research, with a complex array of schools, centers, institutes, and laboratories, the University today seems far removed from that little band of scholars and students who assembled on North Howard Street in Baltimore in the fall of 1876. But it perhaps is not too much to say that Daniel Coit Gilman would understand and approve the latter-day history of the institution he did so much to create. In its devotion to truth, in its emphasis upon quality and creativity, in its dedication to the improvement of the conditions of human beings everywhere, the basic purposes of The Johns Hopkins University have remained constant over the years.

Some Hopkins Dates and Data

1867	Johns Hopkins, a wealthy Quaker merchant, writes his will, incorporating the University and Hospital.
December 24, 1873	Johns Hopkins dies in Baltimore. When his will is probated in January of 1874, his bequests become effective. His fortune of nearly $7 million is divided between the institutions which are to bear his name.
February, 1874	The boards of trustees of the University and Hospital meet for the first time to discuss the best way of carrying out Mr. Hopkins' wishes.
1875	The University's trustees purchase land for the school's first campus. It is in downtown Baltimore, on the west side of North Howard Street near Centre Street.
May 1, 1875	Daniel Coit Gilman assumes the presidency of The Johns Hopkins University. His official inauguration is deferred until February 22 of the following year.
February 22, 1876	The new university, the first of its kind in the United States, officially opens. In the summer that follows, its first Fellows are chosen. Out of 152 applicants, 20 are selected.
October, 1876	Classes begin at the University. The first faculty consists of James Sylvester in mathematics, Basil Gildersleeve in Greek, Henry Rowland in physics, Ira Remsen in chemistry, Henry Martin in biology, and Charles Morris in classics.
November, 1876	Professor Sylvester initiates the *American Journal of Mathematics*, the nation's first scholarly journal. This is quickly followed by Ira Remsen's *American Chemical Journal* (1877) and Professor Gildersleeve's *American Journal of Philology* (1880).
February, 1878	The Johns Hopkins University Press, oldest continuing university press in the nation, is founded.
June, 1878	The first candidates for the Ph.D. at Hopkins are presented to President Gilman. They are Henry C. Adams, Thomas Craig, Josiah Royce, and Ernest Sihler.

1878	Dr. Remsen and his assistant, Constantine Fahlberg, discover saccharin in their Hopkins laboratory.
1880	Dr. Rowland invents the ruled grating machine which produces extremely accurate diffraction gratings, thus revolutionizing spectroscopy.
1882	The college of the University is established. It contains eight divisions leading to the B.A. degree.
1882	The first Hopkins lacrosse team is formed.
1883	The committee to establish the medical school meets for the first time and creates a medical faculty consisting of Ira Remsen in chemistry, Henry Martin in physiology, John Billings in hygiene, and William Welch in pathology.
1883	Woodrow Wilson comes to Hopkins as a graduate student in history and political science. He receives his Ph.D. in 1886, and later becomes the first and only U.S. President to earn such a degree.
1886	The Alumni Association, the first move toward organizing alumni, is created.
1887	Baltimore and Ohio Railroad stock fails. The University owns 15,000 shares and is hurt badly. Tuition is raised and salaries frozen. The citizens of Baltimore come to the University's rescue.
May, 1889	The Johns Hopkins Hospital opens with the "four doctors" (William Welch, William Osler, William Halsted, and Howard Kelly) at the helm. It is one of the first teaching hospitals in the nation.
1889	Dr. Halsted invents the rubber surgical glove.
October, 1889	The Johns Hopkins Training School (School of Nursing) opens with 19 students under the direction of Isabel Hampton.
December, 1892	The completion of the endowment fund for the medical school is brought about by the donation of $100,000 by the Women's Medical School Fund, headed by Mary Garrett. The gift stipulates that women be admitted to the new school on the same basis as men.

October, 1893	The Johns Hopkins Medical School opens with 18 students (3 women) and a faculty of 15. It is not called the School of Medicine until 1924. William Welch is the new school's first dean.
1894	The women's fund memorial building, the first building of the medical school, is completed. It is now known as the Anatomy Building.
1895	The Hopkins chapter of Phi Beta Kappa is founded. Daniel Gilman is the Chapter's first president.
June, 1897	The first doctors graduate from the medical school. There are 15 in the class, 14 men and 1 woman.
1898	The elective system, a major change in medical training, is introduced at the medical school.
1899	The Johns Hopkins Club is organized and opens its doors at 706 St. Paul Street in January of 1900 with Joseph S. Ames as its first president.
Spring, 1901	After 25 years of service, Daniel Gilman, the University's first president, retires. Ira Remsen, professor of chemistry, is elected to succeed him. Remsen's official duties begin on September 1, 1901, but his inauguration is deferred until February 22, 1902, the University's twenty-fifth birthday.
March, 1902	Negotiations to obtain the Homewood Campus are completed. Success in this endeavor is largely due to the efforts of William Keyser and William Wyman.
1905	The Hunterian Laboratory is completed at the medical school. In 1916, it is replaced with a modern structure known as the New Hunterian Laboratory.
1909	The first Master of Arts degree is granted by the University.
1911	The first summer sessions of the University begin.
January, 1912	Maryland appropriates $600,000 plus $50,000 annually to found the School of Engineering. The first students are admitted to the new school in October of 1912.

April, 1912	President Remsen retires, effective January 1, 1913.
June, 1912	The *Johns Hopkins Alumni Magazine* is established. Lawrence C. Writh serves as its first editor.
February, 1914	The University announces that Dr. Frank Goodnow will become its third president.
May, 1915	Gilman Hall, the first building on the Homewood Campus, is dedicated. The dedication of Maryland Hall, the second Homewood building, takes place later the same month. Ground is broken for Latrobe Hall in October of the same year.
1916	The first Reserve Officers Training Corps (R.O.T.C.) in the nation is established at Hopkins.
1917	The world's first School of Hygiene and Public Health, a new division of the University, opens in east Baltimore under the direction of William Welch.
1922	While working at the School of Hygiene, Dr. E. V. McCollum discovers vitamin D. Earlier in his career, he had discovered vitamin A.
June, 1922	Ground is broken at Homewood for the Alumni Memorial Dormitory. The dormitory is occupied in the fall of 1923.
1923	The Pathology Building is completed at the medical school.
1924	The idea of the Walter Hines Page School for the study of international problems is born. The school materializes in 1930, when it opens in Gilman Hall. The Page School ceases to operate in the 1950's.
1924	Remsen Hall, the chemistry building, opens.
February, 1925	President Goodnow announces the Goodnow Plan for the University's future. The Goodnow Plan is approved by the trustees in January of 1926 and calls for the gradual abandonment of undergraduate work. The plan is abolished in 1930.
1925	The School of Hygiene and Public Health Building is completed in east Baltimore.
1926	The idea of the Institute of Law begins to grow. It is planned as a research institute rather than a law

	school, but the Depression claims it as one of its early victims.
1928	Two new medical school buildings are completed: the Wilmer Clinic and the Welch Medical Library.
Spring, 1929	President Frank Goodnow resigns. On July 1, 1929, Joseph Ames becomes the fourth president of the University.
1929	Levering Hall, the YMCA building, opens at Homewood. Rowland Hall, the physics building, is next to be completed. The Physiology Building at the medical school is completed the same year.
June, 1935	President Ames retires. He is succeeded by Isaiah Bowman, who becomes the University's fifth president on July 1, 1935.
1937	A building for the Johns Hopkins Club, the gift of the Marburg family, is completed.
1941	Mergenthaler Hall is completed and houses the Department of Biology.
1942	The Radiation Laboratory is established to carry on research for the Department of Defense under Navy and Air Force sponsorship. The name is changed to the Carlyle Barton Laboratory in 1962. The facility continues to operate until 1970.
1942	The University assumes responsibility for the Applied Physics Laboratory in Silver Spring. The facility had been established by the federal government to develop the variable-time fuze during World War II, a task it successfully completed.
1944	Drs. Alfred Blalock and Helen Taussig perform the first "blue baby" operation, using a dramatic new technique.
1945	The Applied Physics Laboratory produces the first supersonic ramjet engine. A year later, the Laboratory produces the first black and white pictures of the earth taken from space.
1947	All of the evening offerings of the University are consolidated into a new division called McCoy College.

1947	Using techniques developed by Dr. William B. Kouwenhoven, professor of electrical engineering, doctors of The Johns Hopkins Hospital successfully resucitate a patient with a fibrillating heart. In 1957, Dr. Kouwenhoven produces the AC closed chest defibrillator and in 1961, the portable defibrillator becomes a reality.
1948	The Chesapeake Bay Institute is founded to study the ecology of the Bay.
1948	Hopkins produces the first weekly educational television series affiliated with a university. The series, first known as The Johns Hopkins Science Review, is directed by Lynn Poole.
December, 1948	President Bowman resigns. In January of 1949, Detlev Bronk becomes the University's sixth president.
1949	The Department of Biophysics is endowed by Mrs. Thomas Jenkins in honor of her husband. Jenkins Hall is opened the following year.
1950	The University assumes responsibility for a new division, the School of Advanced International Studies, in Washington. The school had been established in 1943 by the U.S. Foreign Service Educational Foundation.
1953	President Bronk resigns to head the Rockefeller Institute. Lowell Reed succeeds him, becoming the University's seventh president.
1954	Three new buildings are completed at Homewood: Shriver Hall, which provides a fine auditorium and housing for certain administrative offices, Ames Hall, which provides space for the departments of Electrical Engineering, Psychology, and Sanitary Engineering, and the new dormitory.
1955	Hopkins establishes a SAIS center in Bologna, Italy. It is the first American graduate school in Europe.
1956	President Reed resigns. Dr. Milton Eisenhower takes his place in the summer of 1956 although he is not formally inaugurated as the eighth president until February 22, 1957.

1957	APL announces the discovery of the Doppler Satellite Tracking System.
1958	Reed Hall west wing is completed at the medical school. Reed Hall east wing is added in 1966. Both wings are residence halls.
1959	Nichols House, the home for the University's president, is completed at Homewood. At the medical school, the Wood Basic Science Building opens.
1959	The Department of Social Relations is established.
1960	The University receives a $6 million grant from the Ford Foundation.
1961	The School of Engineering becomes the School of Engineering Sciences. Civil, Mechanical, and Aeronautical Engineering are combined into a single Department of Mechanics.
1962	Barton Hall and the Carnegie Embryological Laboratory are completed.
1962	The Department of Statistics is established.
1963	The Biophysics Building opens at the medical school.
1963	A Master of Liberal Arts program is initiated in McCoy College.
1964	The History of Science Department is created at the University.
1964	The new Homewood Library is completed. It is named the Milton S. Eisenhower Library in 1965. At the medical school, both the Wood Research Building and the Radiological Science wing of the School of Hygiene and Public Health are completed.
1965	The Newton H. White, Jr. Athletic Center and the Merrick Gateway are completed. Shaffer Hall, which provides much needed classroom space, is completed the same year, although not named for Dean G. Wilson Shaffer until 1967.
1966	Macaulay Hall, the oceanography building, is completed. Dunning Hall, which provides additional

	space for the chemistry department, also opens in 1966. The medical school's animal farm opens in Baltimore county.
1966	The Center for Research in the Social Organization of Schools is established. The Humanities Center begins the same year.
1966	The Faculties of Engineering and Philosophy are combined to form the Faculty of Arts and Sciences.
1966	The gender identity clinic is established at the medical institutions. This leads to the first American "sex change" operation in 1966.
1966	McCoy College's title is changed to The Evening College.
June, 1967	Milton Eisenhower retires. Lincoln Gordon, who is inaugurated on February 22, 1968, is his successor and becomes the University's ninth president.
Fall, 1967	The Academic Council votes to remove credit from all courses taught by the Army R.O.T.C.
1967	The first color pictures of the earth taken from space are produced by an APL satellite.
1968	The Turner Auditorium Building and the Traylor Research Laboratory open at the medical school.
March, 1968	The first annual Milton S. Eisenhower Symposium is held. Its topic is urban affairs.
1968	The Stebbins wing of the School of Hygiene and Public Health Building opens.
1969	The Center for Urban Affairs is created. It is renamed the Center for Metropolitan Planning in 1972.
October, 1969	The Academic Council recommends that female undergraduates be admitted for the 1970-71 school year. This is approved by the board of trustees.
1969	The Steinwald Alumni House opens on North Charles Street.
1971	The Evening College introduces two new programs: the Master of Science (in computer and environmental engineering) and Master of Administrative Science, and discontinues the M.A.T. program begun in 1960.

March, 1971	Lincoln Gordon announces his resignation. By the end of the month, the trustees announce that Milton Eisenhower will once again become president of the University on an interim basis.
Spring, 1971	With Dr. Eisenhower's encouragement, the first recent graduate trustees are appointed to the board.
Fall, 1971	The School of Health Services is created. The first students enter in the fall of 1973.
1971	Garland Hall, the administration building, opens.
January, 1972	The trustees announce that Steven Muller will become the tenth president of the University. He is inaugurated on February 22, 1972.
1972	The Departments of Statistics, Computer Science, and Operations Research are merged to create a new Department of Mathematical Sciences.
February, 1973	President Muller announces the Hopkins Hundreds campaign to raise $100 million by 1976, the University's 100th birthday. Five days later, he announces the first $1 million gift, from the D. Mead Johnson Foundation, to establish a chair in chemistry.
March, 1973	The Evening College opens a center in Columbia, Maryland, and one at Goucher College.
Spring, 1973	A committee composed of members of the Hopkins and Goucher communities is set up to examine the future relationship of the two schools. The committee reports in the fall of 1973 and advocates greater cooperation between the two institutions, but not merger.
1973	APL announces the development of a revolutionary rechargeable heart pacemaker.
February, 1974	Dr. Muller announces that the halfway mark in the Hopkins Hundreds campaign has been reached.
June, 1974	Ground is broken at the medical school for a new complex of buildings to include the Cancer Center, replacement bed facilities, and teaching space.
October, 1974	The Hopkins Union, adjoining Levering Hall, is officially opened.

Library of Congress Cataloging in Publication Data

Sharkey, Robert P.
  Johns Hopkins.

  1. Johns Hopkins University—History. I. Title.
LD2628.S42   378.752'6   74-34210